A SHORT HISTORY OF DECAY

BY E. M. CIORAN

E. M. CIORAN

A Short History of Decay

TRANSLATED FROM THE FRENCH
BY RICHARD HOWARD

FOREWORD BY EUGENE THACKER

ARCADE PUBLISHING • NEW YORK

First published in France under the title *Précis de décomposition*

Arcade Publishing® is a registered trademark of Skyhorse Publishing, Inc.®,
a Delaware corporation.

Visit our website at www.arcadepub.com.

20 19 18 17 16 15 14 13 12

Library of Congress Cataloging-in-Publication Data is available on file.

ISBN: 978-1-61145-736-0
Ebook ISBN: 978-1-62872-494-3

Printed in the United States of America

CONTENTS

FOREWORD

by Eugene Thacker

There are writers that one seeks out, and there are writers that one stumbles upon. Emil Cioran is arguably of the latter kind. Such was my own introduction to his work, as a student meandering one rainy afternoon in a used bookstore in Seattle. In the philosophy section, probably squeezed between "Cicero" and "Confucius," was a book that jumped out simply by its title: *A Short History of Decay*. Spine-creased and slightly dog-eared, it was by an author I knew nothing about. But the title was evocative. Decay, decline, decadence—these are never popular topics, especially in an era such as ours, equally enamored with the explanatory power of science as we are with an almost religious preoccupation with self-help. But how can one write a "short" history of decay? And is there not something contradictory in assembling a "history" of decay? Even the original French title—*Précis de décomposition*—is curious. In French, one often gives the title *Précis* to textbook summaries—for example, a *Précis de littérature française* or a *Précis de mathématiques*. But a "précis" of decay? It seemed absurd to write such a book. And so I bought it.

That used bookstore no longer exists, though I still have my copy of Cioran's book. Originally published in 1949, *A Short History of Decay* was the first book Cioran wrote in French. Born in the small Romanian village of Rășinari in 1911, Cioran attended university in Bucharest, where he discovered the works of Pascal and Nietzsche. While there, he befriended Mircea Eliade and Eugène Ionesco, and while still in his twenties, he published several books in Romanian of impassioned and lyrical prose. He also became enthralled by the turbulent politics of the time, an enthusiasm that eventually gave way to disillusionment and bitterness. In the late 1930s, with the support of the French Institute in Bucharest, Cioran was in Paris, ostensibly to write his philosophy thesis. Instead, he spent many of his days bicycling around France. For Cioran it was a time of intense poverty; not only was it difficult to make ends meet, but he experienced both a cultural and linguistic self-exile, writing in a language not his own, in a style composed entirely of fragments, during the long nights of insomnia that he would struggle with his entire life. In the 1940s, against the backdrop of world war, Cioran began a project originally entitled *Exercices négatifs* (*Negative Exercises*), then *Penseur d'occasion* (*Second-Hand Thinker*), before finally becoming *Précis de décomposition*, or *A Short History of Decay*, in the present translation. The project opened a floodgate in his thinking, resulting in some eight hundred manuscript pages and four different manuscript versions of the book.

When *A Short History of Decay* was published, it tended to polarize readers. Many dismissed it as overly morose and pessimistic, completely out of tune with the obligatory optimism of postwar European culture. Others praised it for precisely these reasons (in his review of the book, Maurice Nadeau proclaimed Cioran "the one whose arrival has been prepared by all the philosophers of the void and of the absurd, harbinger of bad news par excellence"). The original impact of Cioran's book can still be felt in reading *A Short History of Decay* today. Like Nietzsche, Cioran is intent on exposing the hypocrisies of the human condition; but unlike Nietzsche, Cioran never once offers a way out, a new horizon, or even words of inspiration. And yet, there is an enthusiasm in Cioran's prose that comes through, in spite of his predilection towards pessimism and despair: "It is because it rests on nothing, because it lacks even the shadow of an argument that we persevere in life"; "How invent a remedy for existence, how conclude this endless cure? And how recover from your own birth?" There is a kind of ecstasy of the worst

in Cioran's writing that manifests itself in his many voices—
sometimes philosophical, sometimes poetic, sometimes political,
always polemical. *A Short History of Decay* is at once a work
of philosophy and yet a sort of song, a conflicted and agonistic
testament of the "magnificent futility" that is humanity—and
the ambivalence this book expresses is, arguably, more and more
relevant today in our own era of climate change, peak oil, and
disasters both natural and artificial.

Though his books are well-regarded today, and though
he received many literary prizes for them (nearly all of which
he refused), Cioran always held the worlds of literature and
philosophy at arm's length. His willful experiment with style has
largely prevented his work from being easily recognized: neither
philosophy nor poetry, neither essay nor novel, neither manifesto
nor confession. Perhaps he preferred it this way. Of course, in our
digital age is quite easy to find Cioran's books. The real question
is why one would read them. In this sense, perhaps the *only* way
to encounter Cioran is to stumble across him, as if by accident
or by fate.

A SHORT HISTORY OF DECAY

1

DIRECTIONS FOR DECOMPOSITION

Genealogy of Fanaticism—The Anti-Prophet—In the Graveyard of Definitions—Civilization and Frivolity—Dissolving into God—Variations on Death—In the Margin of Moments—Dislocation of Time—Magnificent Futility—Exegesis of Failure—Coalition against Death—Supremacy of the Adjective—The Devil Reassured—Promenade around the Circumference—The Sundays of Life—Resignation—The Indirect Animal—The Key to Our Endurance—Annihilation by Deliverance—The Abstract Venom—The Consciousness of Misery—Interjective Thought—Apotheosis of the Vague—Solitude–Schism of the Heart—Twilight Thinkers—Resources of Self-Destruction—The Reactionary Angels—The Concern for Decency—Gamut of the Void—Certain Mornings—Militant Mourning—Immunity to Renunciation—The World's Equilibrium—Farewell to Philosophy—

From Saint to Cynic—Return to the Elements—
Subterfuges—Non-Resistance to Night—Turning a
Cold Shoulder to Time—Two-Faced Freedom—
Overworked by Dreams—The Model Traitor—In
One of the Earth's Attics—Indefinite Horror—Un-
conscious Dogmas—Duality—The Renegade—
Shades of the Future—The Flower of Fixed Ideas—
The "Celestial Dog"—Ambiguity of Genius—Idola-
try of Disaster—The Demon—The Mockery of a
"New Life"—Triple Impasse—Cosmogony of De-
sire—Interpretation of Actions—Life without Ob-
jective—Acedia—Crimes of Courage and Fear—
Disintoxication—Itinerary of Hate—"La Perduta
Gente"—History and Language—Philosophy and
Prostitution—Obsession of the Essential—Felicity
of Epigones—Ultimate Audacity—Effigy of the Failure—Conditions of Tragedy—The Immanent Lie—
The Coming of Consciousness—The Arrogance
of Prayer—Lypemania—Everyday Curse—Defense
of Corruption—The Obsolete Universe—
Decrepit Man

I'll join with black despair against my soul,
And to myself become an enemy.

—*Richard III*

Genealogy of Fanaticism

In itself, every idea is neutral, or should be; but man animates ideas, projects his flames and flaws into them; impure, transformed into beliefs, ideas take their place in time, take shape as *events*: the trajectory is complete, from logic to epilepsy . . . whence the birth of ideologies, doctrines, deadly games.

Idolaters by instinct, we convert the objects of our dreams and our interests into the Unconditional. History is nothing but a procession of false Absolutes, a series of temples raised to pretexts, a degradation of the mind before the Improbable. Even when he turns from religion, man remains subject to it; depleting himself to create fake gods, he then feverishly adopts them: his need for fiction, for mythology triumphs over evidence and absurdity alike. His power to adore is responsible for all his crimes: a man who loves a god unduly forces other men to love his god, eager to exterminate them if they refuse. There is no form of intolerance, of proselytism or ideological intransigence which fails to reveal the bestial substratum of enthusiasm. Once man loses his *faculty of indifference* he becomes a potential murderer; once he transforms *his* idea into a god the consequences are incalculable. We kill only in the name of a god or of his counterfeits: the excesses provoked by the goddess Reason, by the concept of nation, class, or race are akin to those of the Inquisition or of the Reformation. The ages of fervor abound in bloody exploits: a Saint Teresa could only be the contemporary of the auto-da-fé, a Luther of the repression of the Peasants' Revolt. In every mystic outburst, the moans of victims parallel the moans of ecstasy. . . . Scaffolds, dungeons, jails flourish only in the shadow of a faith—of

3

that need to believe which has infested the mind forever. The devil pales beside the man who owns a truth, *his* truth. We are unfair to a Nero, a Tiberius: it was not they who invented the concept *heretic*: they were only degenerate dreamers who happened to be entertained by massacres. The real criminals are men who establish an orthodoxy on the religious or political level, men who distinguish between the faithful and the schismatic.

When we refuse to admit the interchangeable character of ideas, blood flows . . . firm resolves draw the dagger; fiery eyes presage slaughter. No wavering mind, infected with Hamletism, was ever pernicious: the principle of evil lies in the will's tension, in the incapacity for quietism, in the Promethean megalomania of a race that bursts with ideals, that explodes with its convictions, and that, in return for having forsaken doubt and sloth—vices nobler than all its virtues—has taken the path to perdition, into history, that indecent alloy of banality and apocalypse. . . . Here certitudes abound: suppress them, best of all suppress their consequences, and you recover paradise. What is the Fall but the pursuit of a truth and the assurance you have found it, the passion for a dogma, domicile within a dogma? The result is fanaticism—fundamental defect which gives man the craving for effectiveness, for prophecy, for terror—a lyrical leprosy by which he contaminates souls, subdues them, crushes or exalts them. . . . Only the skeptics (or idlers or aesthetes) escape, because they *propose* nothing, because they—humanity's true bene-factors—undermine fanaticism's purposes, analyze its frenzy. I feel *safer* with a Pyrrho than with a Saint Paul, for a jesting wisdom is gentler than an unbridled sanctity. In the fervent mind you always find the camouflaged beast of prey; no protection is adequate against the claws of a prophet. . . . Once he raises his voice, whether in the name of heaven, of the city, or some other excuse, away with you: satyr of your solitude, he will not forgive your living on the wrong side of his truths and his transports; he wants you to share his hysteria, his fullness, he wants to impose it on you, and thereby to disfigure you. A human being possessed by a belief and not eager to pass it on to others is a phenomenon alien to the earth, where our mania for salvation makes life unbreathable. Look around you: everywhere, specters preaching; each institution translates a mission;

city halls have their absolute, even as the temples—officialdom, with its rules—a metaphysics designed for monkeys. . . . Everyone trying to remedy everyone's life: even beggars, even the incurable aspire to it: the sidewalks and hospitals of the world overflow with reformers. The longing to become a source of *events* affects each man like a mental disorder or a desired malediction. Society—an inferno of saviors! What Diogenes was looking for with his lantern was an *indifferent man*. . . .

It is enough for me to hear someone talk sincerely about ideals, about the future, about philosophy, to hear him say "we" with a certain inflection of assurance, to hear him invoke "others" and regard himself as their interpreter—for me to consider him my enemy. I see in him a tyrant *manqué*, an approximate executioner, quite as detestable as the first-rate tyrants, the first-rate executioners. Every faith practices some form of terror, all the more dreadful when the "pure" are its agents. We mistrust the swindler, the trickster, the con man; yet to them we can impute none of history's great convulsions; believing in nothing, it is not they who rummage in your hearts, or your ulterior motives; they leave you to your apathy, to your despair or to your uselessness; to them humanity owes the few moments of prosperity it has known: it is they who save the peoples whom fanatics torture and "idealists" destroy. Doctrineless, they have only whims and interests, accommodating vices a thousand times more endurable than the ravages provoked by principled despotism; for all of life's evils come from a "conception of life." An accomplished politician should search out the ancient sophists and take lessons in oratory—and in corruption. . . .

Whereas the fanatic is incorruptible: if he kills for an idea, he can just as well get himself killed for one; in either case, tyrant or martyr, he is a monster. No human beings more dangerous than those who have suffered for a belief: the great persecutors are recruited among the martyrs not quite beheaded. Far from diminishing the appetite for power, suffering exasperates it; hence the mind feels more comfortable in the society of a braggart than in that of a martyr; and nothing is more repugnant to it than the spectacle of dying for an idea. . . . Revolted by the sublime and by carnage, the mind dreams of a provincial ennui *on the scale of the universe*, of a

History whose stagnation would be so great that doubt would take on the lineaments of an event and hope a calamity. . . .

The Anti-Prophet

In every man sleeps a prophet, and when he wakes there is a little more evil in the world. . . .

The compulsion to preach is so rooted in us that it emerges from depths unknown to the instinct for self-preservation. Each of us awaits *his* moment in order to propose something—anything. He has a voice: that is enough. It costs us dear to be neither deaf nor dumb. . . .

From snobs to scavengers, all expend their criminal generosity, all hand out formulas for happiness, all try to give directions: life in common thereby becomes intolerable, and life with oneself still more so; if you fail to meddle in other people's business you are so uneasy about your own that you convert your "self" into a religion, or, apostle in reverse, you deny it altogether; we are victims of the universal game. . . .

The abundance of solutions to the aspects of existence is equaled only by their futility. History: a factory of ideals . . . lunatic mythology, frenzy of hordes and of solitaries . . . refusal to look reality in the face, mortal thirst for fictions. . . .

The source of our actions resides in an unconscious propensity to regard ourselves as the center, the cause, and the conclusion of time. Our reflexes and our pride transform into a planet the parcel of flesh and consciousness we are. If we had the right sense of our position in the world, if *to compare* were inseparable from *to live*, the revelation of our infinitesimal presence would crush us. But to live is to blind ourselves to our own dimensions. . . .

And if all our actions—from breathing to the founding of empires or metaphysical systems—derive from an illusion as to our importance, the same is true a fortiori of the prophetic instinct. Who, with the exact vision of his nullity, would try to be effective and to turn himself into a savior?

Nostalgia for a world without "ideals," for an agony without doctrine, for an eternity without life . . . Paradise. . . . But we could not exist one second without deceiving ourselves: the prophet in each of us is just the seed of madness which makes us flourish in our void.

The ideally lucid, hence ideally *normal,* man should have no recourse beyond the *nothing* that is in him. . . . I can imagine him saying: "Torn from the goal, from all goals, I retain, of my desires and my displeasures, only their formulas. Having resisted the temptation to conclude, I have overcome the mind, as I have overcome life itself by the horror of looking for an answer to it. The spectacle of man—what an emetic! Love—a duel of salivas. . . . All the feelings milk their absolute from the misery of the glands. Nobility is only in the negation of existence, in a smile that surveys annihilated landscapes. Once I had a 'self'; now I am no more than an object . . . I gorge myself on all the drugs of solitude; those of the world were too weak to make me forget it. Having killed the prophet in me, how could I still have a place among men?"

In the Graveyard of Definitions

Are we entitled to imagine a mind exclaiming: "Everything is purposeless to me now, for I have given the definitions of all things"? And if we could imagine such a mind, how locate it within duration?

What surrounds us we endure better for giving it a name—and moving on. But to embrace a thing by a definition, however arbitrary—and all the more serious the more arbitrary it is, since the soul then overtakes knowledge—is to reject that thing, to render it insipid and superfluous, to annihilate it. The idle, empty mind—which joins the world only by the grace of sleep—can practice only by extending the name of things, by emptying them and substituting formulas for them. Then it maneuvers over their debris; no more sensations; nothing but memories. Under each formula lies a corpse: being and object alike die under the pretext they have occasioned. This is the mind's frivolous, funereal debauch. And this mind has squandered itself in what it has named and circumscribed. Infatuated by syllables, it loathed the mystery of heavy silences and turned them light and pure; and it too has become light and pure, indeed lightened and purified of everything. The vice of defining has made it a gracious assassin, and a discreet victim.

This is how the stain the soul spread over the mind has been removed—the only thing which reminded it that it was alive.

Civilization and Frivolity

How could we bear the weight and sheer depth of works and masterpieces, if to their texture certain impertinent and delicious minds had not added the fringes of subtle scorn and ready ironies? And how could we endure the codes, the customs, the paragraphs of the heart which inertia and propriety have superimposed upon the futile and intelligent vices, if it were not for those playful beings whose refinement puts them at once at the apex and in the margin of society?

We must be thankful to the civilizations which have not taken an overdose of seriousness, which have played with values and taken their pleasure in begetting and destroying them. Who knows, outside of the Greek and French civilizations, a more lucidly facetious proof of the elegant nothingness of things? The age of Alcibiades and the eighteenth century in France are two sources of consolation. While it is only at their final stages, at the dissolution of a whole system of behavior and belief, that the other civilizations could enjoy that lively exercise which lends a flavor of futility to life, it was in full ripeness, in full possession of their powers and of the future that these two epochs knew the tedium heedless of everything and permeable to everything. What better symbol than that of Madame du Deffand, old, blind, and perspicacious, who even while execrating life, nonetheless relished to the last its every amenity of gall?

No one achieves frivolity straight off. It is a privilege and an art; it is the pursuit of the superficial by those who, having discerned the impossibility of any certitude, have conceived a disgust for such things; it is the escape far from one abyss or another which, being by nature bottomless, can lead nowhere.

There remain, nonetheless, the appearances; why not raise them to the level of a *style*? Thereby we define every intelligent period. Thereby we find more prestige in expression than in the soul which supports it, in grace than in intuition; emotion itself becomes polite. The human being delivered to himself, without any partiality for elegance, is a monster; he finds only dark regions there, where terror and negation, imminent, prowl. To know, by all one's vitality, that one will die, and to be unable to conceal it, is an act of barbarism. Any *sincere* philosophy renounces the claims of civilization, whose function consists in sifting our secrets and disguising them as *recherché* effects. Thus, frivolity is the most effective antidote to the disease of being what one is: by frivolity we abuse the world and dissimulate the impropriety of our depths. Without its artifices, how could we help blushing to have a soul? Our skin-deep solitudes, what an inferno for other people! But it is always for them, and sometimes for ourselves, that we invent our appearances. . . .

Dissolving into God

The mind scrupulous of its distinct essence is threatened at every turn by the things it rejects. Often abandoning attention—the greatest of its privileges—such a mind yields to the temptations it has sought to escape, or becomes the prey of impure mysteries. . . . Who has not known those fears, those dizzy spells, those deliriums which bring us back to the beast, back to the last problems? Our knees tremble but do not bend; our hands clutch without clasping each other; our eyes look up and see nothing. . . . We preserve that vertical pride which strengthens its courage; that horror of gestures which saves us from spectacle; and the succor of eyelids to veil an absurdly ineffable gaze. Our collapse is imminent but not inevitable; the accident is odd, but scarcely new; already a smile dawns on the horizon of our terrors . . . we shall not topple into prayer. . . . For after all *He* must not triumph; it is up to our irony to compromise His capital letter; up to our heart to dissolve the shudders He dispenses.

If such a Being really existed, if our weaknesses vanquished our resolutions and our depths our deliberations, then why go on thinking, since our difficulties would be settled, our questions suspended, and our fears allayed? Which would be too easy. Every absolute—personal or abstract—is a way of avoiding the problems, and not only the problems, but also their root, which is nothing but a panic of the senses.

God: a perpendicular fall upon our fear, a salvation landing like a thunderbolt amid our investigations which no hope deceives, the immediate annihilation of our unconsoled and determinedly inconsolable pride, a sidetracking of the individual, the soul on the dole for lack of anxiety. . . .

What greater renunciation than Faith? True, without it we are committed to an infinity of dead ends. But even when we know that nothing leads anywhere, that the universe is only a by-product of our gloom, why should we sacrifice this pleasure of tottering and of splitting our skulls against heaven and earth?

The solutions offered by our ancestral cowardice are the worst desertions of our duty to intellectual decency. To be fooled, to live and die *duped,* is certainly what men do. But there exists a dignity which keeps us from disappearing into God and which transforms all our moments into prayers we shall never offer.

Variations on Death

I. It is because it rests on nothing, because it lacks even the shadow of an argument that we persevere in life. Death is too exact; it has all the reasons on its side. Mysterious for our instincts, it takes shape, to our reflection, limpid, without glamor, and without the false lures of the unknown.

By dint of accumulating non-mysteries and monopolizing non-meanings, life inspires more dread than death: it is life which is the Great Unknown.

Where can so much Void and Incomprehensibility lead? We cling to the days because the desire to die is too logical, hence ineffective. If life had a single argument in its favor—distinct, indisputable—it would annihilate itself; instincts and prejudices collapse at the contact of Rigor. Everything that breathes feeds on the unverifiable; a dose of logic would be deadly to existence—that effort toward the Senseless. . . . Give life a specific goal and it immediately loses its attraction. The inexactitude of its ends makes life superior to death; one touch of precision would degrade it to the triviality of the tombs. For a positive science of the meaning of life would depopulate the earth in a day, and not even a madman could succeed in reviving the fruitful improbability of Desire.

II. Men can be classified according to the most whimsical criteria: according to their humors, their inclinations, their dreams, or their glands. We change ideas like neckties; for every idea, every criterion comes from outside, from the configurations and accidents of time. But there is something that comes from ourselves, that *is* ourselves, an invisible but inwardly verifiable reality, an unwonted and eternal presence that we can conceive at any moment and that we never dare admit, which is real only before its consummation: death, the true criterion. . . . And it is death, the most intimate dimension of all the living, which separates humanity into two orders so irreducible, so removed from each other, that there is more distance between them than between a vulture and a mole, a star and a starfish. The abyss of two incommunicable worlds opens between the man who has the sentiment of death and the man who does not; yet both die; but one is unaware of his death, the other *knows*; one dies only for a moment, the other unceasingly. . . . Their common condition locates them precisely at each other's antipodes, at the two extremities and within one and the same definition; irreconcilable, they suffer the same fate. . . . One lives as if he were eternal; the other thinks continually of his eternity and denies it in each thought.

Nothing can change our life but the gradual insinuation within us of the forces which annihilate it. No new principle comes to it from the surprises of our growth nor from the efflorescence of our gifts; they are merely natural to it. And nothing natural can make us anything but ourselves.

Everything which prefigures death adds a quality of novelty to life, modifies and amplifies it. Health preserves life as such, in a sterile identity; while disease is an activity, the most intense a man can indulge in, a frenetic and . . . stationary movement, the richest expenditure of energy *without gesture*, the hostile and impassioned expectation of an irreparable lightning bolt.

III. Against the obsession with death, both the subterfuges of hope and the arguments of reason lay down their arms: their insignificance merely whets the appetite to die. In order to triumph over this appetite, there is but one "method": to live it to the end, to submit to all its pleasures, all its pangs, to do nothing to elude it. An obsession experienced to the point of satiety is annihilated in its own excesses. By dwelling on the infinity of death, thought manages to *use it up*, to inspire disgust for it in us, disgust, that *negative* superfluity which spares nothing and which, before compromising and diminishing the prestige of death, shows us the inanity of life.

The man who has not given himself up to the pleasures of anguish, who has not savored in his mind the dangers of his own extinction nor relished such cruel and sweet annihilations, will never be cured of the obsession with death: he will be tormented by it, for he will have resisted it; while the man who, habituated to a discipline of horror, and meditating upon his own carrion, has deliberately reduced himself to ashes—that man will look toward death's *past*, and he himself will be *merely a resurrected being who can no longer live*. His "method" will have cured him of both life and death.

Every crucial experience is fatal: the layers of existence lack density; the man who explores them, archaeologist of the heart, of being, finds himself, at the end of his researches, confronting *empty depths*. He will vainly regret the panoply of appearances.

Hence the ancient Mysteries, so-called revelations of the ultimate secrets, have bequeathed us nothing by way of knowledge. The initiates were doubtless obliged to keep silence; yet it is inconceivable that not a single chatterbox was among their number; what is more contrary to human nature than such stubbornness in secrecy? The fact is that there were no *secrets*; there were rites, there were shudders. Once the veils had fallen, what could they discover but insignificant consequences? *The only initiation is to nothingness— and to the mockery of being alive.* . . . And I dream of an Eleusis of disabused hearts, of a lucid Mystery, without gods and without the vehemences of illusion.

In the Margin of Moments

It is our incapacity to weep which sustains our taste for things, which makes them exist at all: it keeps us from exhausting their savor and from turning away. When, on so many brinks and byroads, our eyes refused to drown in themselves, their dryness preserved the object which amazed them. Our tears squander nature, as our terrors do God . . . but in the end, they squander ourselves. For we *exist* only by the refusal to give free rein to our supreme desires: the things which enter the sphere of our admiration or our despair remain there only because we have neither sacrificed them nor blessed them with our liquid farewells.

So it is that after each night, facing a new day, the impossible necessity of dealing with it fills us with dread; exiled in light as if the world had just started, inventing the sun, we flee from tears—just one of which would be enough to wash us out of time.

Dislocation of Time

The moments follow each other; nothing lends them the illusion of a content or the appearance of a meaning; they pass; their course is not ours; we contemplate that passage, prisoners of a stupid perception. The heart's void confronting time's: two mirrors, reflecting each other's absence, one and the same image of nullity. . . . As though by the effect of a dreamy idiocy, everything is leveled: no more peaks, no more plunges. . . . Where to locate the poetry of lies, the goad of an enigma?

The man who knows nothing of ennui is still in the world's childhood, when the ages were waiting to be born; he remains closed off from that tired time which outlives itself, which laughs at its dimensions, and succumbs on the threshold of its own . . . future, dragging along matter, suddenly raised to a lyricism of negation. Ennui is the echo in us of time tearing itself apart . . . the revelation of the void, the drying up of that delirium which sustains—or invents—life. . . .

Creator of values, man is the delirious creature *par excellence*, victim of the belief that something exists, whereas he need merely hold his breath: everything stops; suspend his emotions: nothing stirs; suppress his whims: the world turns to ashes. Reality is a creation of our excesses, of our disproportions and derangements. Rein in your palpitations and the course of events slows down; without our ardors, space is ice. Time itself passes only because our desires beget that decorative universe which a jot of lucidity would lay bare. One touch of clearsightedness reduces us to our primal state: nakedness; a suspicion of irony strips us of that trumpery hope which let us dupe ourselves and devise illusion: every contrary path leads outside of life. Ennui is merely the beginning of such an itinerary. . . . It makes us find time long, too long—unsuited to show us an end. Detached from every object, having nothing external to assimilate, we destroy ourselves in slow motion, since the future has stopped offering us a *raison d'être*.

Ennui shows us an eternity which is not the transcendence of time, but its wreck; it is the infinity of souls that have rotted for lack of superstitions, a banal absolute where nothing any longer keeps things from turning in circles, in search of their own Fall.

Life creates itself in delirium and is undone in ennui.

(The man suffering from a characterized sickness is not entitled to complain: he has an occupation. The great sufferers are never bored: disease fills them, the way remorse feeds the great criminals. For any intense suffering produces a simulacrum of plenitude and proposes a terrible reality to consciousness, which it cannot elude; while suffering without *substance* in that temporal mourning of ennui affords consciousness nothing that forces it to fruitful action. How to cure an unlocalized and supremely impalpable disease which infects the body without leaving any trace upon it, which insinuates itself into the soul without marking it by any sign? Ennui is like a sickness we have survived, but one which has absorbed our possibilities, our reserves of *attention* and has left us impotent to fill the void which follows upon the disappearance of our pangs and the fading of our torments. Hell is a haven next to this displacement in time, this empty and prostrate languor in which nothing stops us but the spectacle of the universe decaying before our eyes.

What therapeutics to invoke against a disease we no longer remember and whose aftermath encroaches upon our days? How invent a remedy for existence, how conclude this endless cure? And how recover from your own birth?

Ennui, that *incurable* convalescence . . .)

Magnificent Futility

With the exception of the Greek skeptics and the Roman emperors of the Decadence, all minds seem enslaved by a municipal vocation. Only these two groups are emancipated, the former by doubt, the latter by dementia, from the insipid obsession of being useful. Having promoted the arbitrary to the rank of drill or delirium, depending on whether they were philosophers or disabused scions of the old conquerors, they were attached to nothing: in this regard, they suggest the saints. But while the saints were never to collapse, these others found themselves at the mercy of their own game, masters and victims of their whims—true solitaries, since their solitude was sterile. No one has followed their example and they themselves proposed no such thing; hence they communicated with their "kind" only by irony and terror. . . .

To be the dissolvent of a philosophy or of an empire: what pride could be more melancholy and more majestic? To kill, on the one hand, truth, and greatness on the other, manias which nourish the mind and the city; to undermine the architecture of the façades protecting the thinker's pride and the citizen's; to flex to the point of fracturing the springs of their impulse to conceive and to will; to discredit, by the subtleties of sarcasm and torture, both traditional abstractions and honorable customs—what delicate and brutal effervescence! Nothing beguiles where the gods die before our eyes. In Rome, where they were replaced, imported, where they could be seen to wither, what pleasure to invoke ghosts with yet the one fear that this sublime versatility might capitulate to the assault of some severe and impure deity . . . which is what happened.

It is not easy to destroy an idol: it takes as much time as is required to promote and to worship one. For it is not enough to annihilate its material symbol, which is easy; but its roots in the soul. How turn your eyes toward the twilight ages—when the past was liquidated under a scrutiny which only the void could dazzle—without being moved by that great art which is the death of a civilization?

. . . And so I dream of having been one of those slaves, coming from an improbable country, barbarous and brooding, to languish in the agony of Rome, my vague desolation embellished by Greek sophistries. In the vacant eyes of the statues, in the idols shrunken by sagging superstitions, I should have forgotten all about my ancestors, my yokes, and my regrets. Espousing the melancholy of the ancient symbols, I should have liberated myself; I should have shared the dignity of the abandoned gods, defending them against the insidious crosses, against the invasion of servants and martyrs, and my nights would have sought their rest in the delirium and debauchery of the Caesars. Expert in disillusions, riddling the new fervors with all the arrows of a dissolute wisdom—among the courtesans, in skeptical brothels or circuses with their sumptuous cruelties, I should have swelled my reasonings with vice and with blood, dilating logic to dimensions it had never dreamed of, to the dimensions of worlds that die.

Exegesis of Failure

Each of us is born with a share of purity, predestined to be corrupted by our commerce with mankind, by that sin against solitude. For each of us will do anything in order not to be doomed to himself. Our kind is not a fatality but the temptation to fail. Incapable of keeping our hands clean and our hearts undiluted, we soil ourselves upon contact with strange sweats, we wallow—craving for disgust and fervent for pestilence—in the unanimous mud. And when we dream of seas changed into holy water, it is too late to dive into them, and our advanced state of corruption keeps us from drowning there:

the world has infested our solitude; upon us the traces of others become indelible.

In the gamut of creatures, only man inspires a sustained disgust. The repugnance which an animal begets is provisional; it never ripens in thought, whereas our kind obsesses our reflections, infiltrates the mechanism of our detachment from the world in order to confirm us in our system of refusal and non-adherence. After each conversation, whose refinement alone is enough to indicate the level of a civilization, why is it impossible not to regret the Sahara and not to envy the plants or the endless monologues of zoology?

If with each word we win a victory over nothingness, it is only the better to endure its reign. We die in proportion to the words which we fling around us. . . . Those who speak have no secrets. And we all speak. We betray ourselves, we exhibit our heart; executioner of the unspeakable, each of us labors to destroy all the mysteries, beginning with our own. And if we meet others, it is to degrade ourselves together in a race to the void, whether in the exchange of ideas, schemes, or confessions. Curiosity has provoked not only the first fall but the countless ones of every day of our lives. Life is only that impatience to fall, to fail, to prostitute the soul's virginal solitudes by dialogue, ageless and everyday negation of Paradise. Man should listen only to himself in the endless ecstasy of the intransmissible Word, should create words for his own silences and assents audible only to his regrets. But he is the chatterbox of the universe; he speaks in the name of others; his self loves the plural. And anyone who speaks in the name of others is always an impostor. Politicians, reformers, and all who rely on a collective pretext are cheats. There is only the artist whose lie is not a total one, for he invents only himself. Outside of the surrender to the incommunicable, the suspension amid our mute and unconsoled anxieties, life is merely a fracas on an unmapped terrain, and the universe a geometry stricken with epilepsy.

(The implicit plural of "one" and the avowed plural of "we" constitute the comfortable refuge of false existence. Only the poet takes responsibility for "I," he alone speaks in his own name, he alone is entitled to do so. Poetry is bastardized when it becomes permeable to prophecy or to doctrine: "mission" smothers music, idea shackles inspiration. Shelly's "generous" aspect cripples most of his work; Shakespeare, by a stroke of luck, never "served" anything.

The victory of non-authenticity is fulfilled in philosophical activity, that complacence in "one," and in prophetic activity [whether religious, moral, or political], that apotheosis of "we." *Definition* is the lie of the abstract mind; *inspired formula* the lie of the militant one; a definition is always the cornerstone of a temple; a formula inescapably musters the faithful. Thus all teachings begin.

How then fail to turn to poetry? It has, like life, the excuse of *proving* nothing.)

Coalition against Death

How imagine other people's lives, when our own seems scarcely conceivable? We meet someone, we see him plunged into an impenetrable and unjustifiable world, in a mass of desires and convictions superimposed on reality like a morbid structure. Having made a system of mistakes for himself, he suffers for reasons whose nullity alarms the mind and surrenders himself to values whose absurdity leaps to the eye. What are his undertakings but trifles, and is the feverish symmetry of his concerns any better built than an architecture of twaddle? To the outside observer, the absolute of each life looks interchangeable, and every fate, however fixed in its essence, arbitrary. When our convictions seem the fruit of a frivolous lunacy, how tolerate other people's passions for themselves and for their own multiplication in each day's utopia? By what necessity does this man shut himself up in a particular world of predilections, and that man in another?

When we endure the confidences of a friend or a stranger, the revelation of his secrets fills us with astonishment. Are we to relate his torments to drama or to farce? This depends entirely on the good will or the exasperations of our lassitude. Each fate being no more than a refrain fluttering around a few bloodstains, it is up to our moods to see in the disposition of such sufferings a superfluous and piquant order, or a pretext for pity.

Since it is difficult to approve the reasons people invoke, each time we leave one of our *fellow men*, the question which comes to mind is invariably the same: how does he keep from killing himself? For nothing is more natural than to imagine other people's suicide. When we have glimpsed, by an overwhelming and readily renewable intuition, *anyone's* own uselessness, it is incomprehensible that everyone has not done the same. To do away with oneself seems such a clear and simple action! Why is it so rare, why does everyone avoid it? Because, if reason disavows the appetite for life, the *nothing* which extends our acts is nonetheless of a power superior to all absolutes; it explains the tacit coalition of mortals against death; it is not only the symbol of existence, but existence itself; it is everything. And this nothing, this everything, cannot give life a meaning, but it nonetheless makes life persevere in what it is: *a state of non-suicide.*

Supremacy of the Adjective

Since there can be only a limited number of ways to face the ultimate problems, the mind is limited in its expansion by that natural boundary which is *the essential*, by that impossibility of indefinitely multiplying the capital difficulties: history is solely concerned with changing the aspect of a sum of questions and solutions. What the mind invents is merely a series of new qualifications; it rebaptizes the elements or seeks in its lexicons less eroded epithets for the one immutable pain. We have always suffered, but our suffering has been either "sublime" or "legitimate" or "absurd," according to the general views which the philosophic moment maintained. Misery constitutes the texture of all that breathes; but its modalities have changed course; they have composed that series of irreducible appearances which lead each of us to believe he is the first to have suffered so. The pride of such uniqueness incites us to cherish our own pain and to endure it. In a world of sufferings, each of them is a solipsist in relation to all the rest. Misery's originality is due to the verbal quality which isolates it in the sum of words and sensations. . . .

The qualifiers change: this change is called intellectual progress.

Suppress them all and what would remain of civilization? The difference between intelligence and stupidity resides in the manipulation of the adjective, whose use without diversity constitutes banality. God Himself lives only by the adjectives we add to Him; whereby the *raison d'être* of theology. Hence man, by modulating the monotony of his misery ever variously, justifies himself to the mind only by the impassioned search for a new adjective.

(And yet this search is pitiable. The poverty of *expression*, which is the mind's poverty, is manifest in the indigence of words, in their exhaustion and their degradation: the attributes by which we determine things and sensations finally lie before us like so much verbal carrion. And we glance regretfully at the time when they gave off no more than an odor of confinement. All Alexandrianism begins with the need to *ventilate* words, to make up for their blemishes by a lively refinement; but it ends in a lassitude in which mind and word are mingled and decompose. [Ideally, the final stage of a literature and of a civilization: imagine a Valéry with the soul of a Nero. . . .]

So long as our untried senses and our naïve heart recognize themselves and delight in the universe of qualifications, they flourish with the aid and at the risk of the adjective, which, once dissected, proves inadequate, deficient. We say of space, of time, and of suffering that they are infinite; but *infinite* has no more bearing than beautiful, sublime, harmonious, ugly. . . . Suppose we force ourselves to see to the bottom of words? We see nothing—each of them, detached from the expansive and fertile soul, being null and void. The power of the intelligence functions by projecting a certain luster upon them, by polishing them and making them glitter; this power, erected into a system, is called *culture*—pyrotechnics against a night sky of nothingness.)

The Devil Reassured

Why is God so dull, so feeble, so inadequately picturesque? Why does He lack interest, vigor, actuality and resemble us so little? Is there any image less anthropomorphic and more gratuitously remote?

How could we have projected into Him lights so dim and powers so unsteady? Where have our energeis leaked away to, where have our desires run out? Who then has absorbed our overflow of vital insolence?

Shall we turn to the Devil? But we cannot address our prayers to him: to worship him would be to pray introspectively, to pray to *ourselves*. We do not pray to what is the evidence: the *exact* is not an object of worship. We have placed in our double all our attributes, and, in order to afford him a semblance of solemnity, we have dressed him in black: our vices and our virtues in mourning. By endowing him with wickedness and perseverance, our dominant qualities, we have exhausted ourselves to make him as lively as possible; our powers have been used up in creating his image, in making him agile, frisky, intelligent, ironic, and above all petty. The reserves of energy we still had left to produce God were reduced to nothing. Then we resorted to the imagination and to what little blood we had left: God could be only the fruit of our anemia: a tottering and rachitic image. He is mild, good, sublime, just. But who recognizes himself in that mixture redolent of rose water, relegated to transcendence? A Being without duplicity lacks depth, lacks mystery; He hides nothing. Only impurity is a sign of reality. And if the saints are not completely stripped of interest, it is because their sublimity is tinged with the novelistic, their eternity lends itself to biography; their *lives* indicate that they have left the world for a *genre* capable of captivating us from time to time. . . .

Because he overflows with life, the Devil has no altar: man recognizes himself too readily in him to worship him; he detests him for good reason; he repudiates *himself*, and maintains the indigent attributes of God. But the Devil never complains and never aspires to found a religion: are we not here to safeguard him from inanition and oblivion?

Promenade around the Circumference

Within the circle which encloses human beings in a community of interests and hopes, the mind opposed to mirages clears a path from the center toward the periphery. It can no longer hear at close range the hum of humanity; it wants to consider from as far away as possible the accursed symmetry which links men together. It sees martyrs everywhere: some sacrificing themselves for visible needs, others for inestimable necessities, all ready to bury their names under a certitude; and, since not all of them can succeed, the majority expiate by banality the overflow of blood they have dreamed of . . . their lives consist of an enormous freedom to die which they have not taken advantage of: inexpressive holocaust of history, the boneyard swallows them up.

But the enthusiast of separations, seeking paths unhaunted by the hordes, withdraws to the extreme margin and follows the rim of the circle, which he cannot cross so long as he is subject to the body; yet Consciousness soars farther, quite pure in an ennui without beings or objects. No longer suffering, superior to the excuses which invite dying, Consciousness forgets the man who supports it. More unreal than a star glimpsed in some hallucination, it suggests the condition of a sidereal pirouette—while on life's circumference the soul promenades, meeting only itself over and over again, itself and its impotence to answer the call of the Void.

The Sundays of Life

If Sunday afternoons were extended for months, where would humanity get to, liberated from sweat, from the weight of the first curse? The experiment would be worth the trouble. It is more than likely that crime would become the sole diversion, that debauchery would seem candor, shouting melody and jeers tenderness. The sensation of time's immensity would make each second into an intolerable torment, a sublime firing squad. In hearts imbued with poetry would appear a blasé cannibalism and a hyena's melancholy; butchers and executioners would die out—of lethargy; churches and brothels would split with sighs. *The universe transformed into a Sunday afternoon* . . . it is the very definition of ennui, and the end of the universe. . . . Take away the curse hanging over History and it immediately vanishes, like existence itself, in absolute vacancy, exposing its fiction. Labor builds on nothingness, creates and consolidates myths; elementary intoxication, it excites and maintains the belief in "reality"; but contemplation of pure existence, contemplation independent of actions and objects, assimilates only what is not. . . .

The idle apprehend more things, are deeper than the industrious: no task limits their horizon; born into an eternal Sunday, they watch—and watch themselves watching. Sloth is a somatic skepticism, the way the flesh doubts. In a world of inaction, the idle would be the only ones not to be murderers. But they do not belong to humanity, and, sweat not being their strong point, they live without suffering the consequences of Life and of Sin. Doing neither good nor evil, they disdain—spectators of the human convulsion—the weeks of time, the efforts which asphyxiate consciousness. What would they have to fear from a limitless extension of certain afternoons except the regret of having supported a crudely elementary obviousness? Then, exasperation in the truth might induce them to imitate the others and to indulge in the degrading temptation of tasks. This is the danger which threatens sloth, that miraculous residue of paradise.

(Love's one function is to help us endure those cruel and incommensurable Sunday afternoons which torment us for the rest of the week—and for eternity.

Without the allurement of the ancestral spasm, we should require a thousand eyes for hidden tears, or else nails to bite, mile-long nails. . . . How else kill this time which no longer passes? On those interminable Sundays the *disease of being* is utterly plain. Sometimes we manage to forget ourselves in something; but how forget ourselves in the world itself? This impossibility is the definition of the disease. The man who is afflicted by it will never be cured, even if the universe changed altogether. Only his heart should change, but it is unchangeable; hence for him, *to exist* has only one meaning: to dive into suffering—until the exercise of a day-by-day nirvanization raises him to the perception of unreality. . . .)

Resignation

It was in a clinic waiting room: an old woman was telling me about her diseases. . . . The controversies of men, the hurricanes of history—in her eyes, trifles: her sickness alone prevailed over time and space. "I can't eat, I can't sleep, I'm afraid, there must be some pus here . . ." she began, caressing her jaw with more interest than if the fate of the world depended on it. At first this excess of self-concern on the part of a decrepit crone left me torn between dread and disgust; then I left the clinic before it was my turn, determined to *renounce* my discomforts forever. . . .

"Fifty-nine seconds out of each of my minutes," I reflected as I walked through the streets, "were dedicated to suffering or to . . . the idea of suffering. If only I had a stone's vocation! A *heart*: origin of every torment . . . I aspire to the object, to the blessing of matter and opacity. The zigzagging of a gnat seems to me an apocalyptic enterprise. It is a sin to get outside yourself. . . . The wind—air's insanity! Music, the madness of silence! By capitulating to life, this world has betrayed nothingness. . . . I resign from movement, and from my dreams. Absence! You shall be my sole glory. . . . Let "desire" be forever stricken from the dictionary, and from the soul! I retreat before the dizzying farce of tomorrows. And if I still cling to a few hopes, I have lost forever the *faculty of hoping*."

The Indirect Animal

What a downfall, when you bear in mind, by some radical obsession, that man exists, that he is what he is—and that he cannot be otherwise. But *what he is* a thousand definitions expose and none compels recognition: the more arbitrary they are, the more valid they seem. The airiest absurdity and the weightiest banality are equally appropriate. The infinity of his attributes composes the most imprecise being we can conceive. Whereas the animals proceed directly to their goal, man loses himself in detours; he is the indirect animal *par excellence*. His improbable reflexes—from whose slackening consciousness derives—transform him into a convalescent aspiring to disease. Nothing in him is healthy except the fact of having been so. Whether he is an angel that has lost his wings or an ape that has lost his hair, he has been able to leave the anonymity of creatures only by the eclipses of his health. His poorly constituted blood has allowed the infiltration of uncertainties, approximations, problems; his wavering vitality, the intrusion of question marks and exclamation points. How define the virus which, eroding his somnolence, has stunned him with insomnia among the universal siesta? What worm has burrowed into his repose, what primal agent of knowledge has forced him to the backwardness of actions, the arrested development of desires? Who has introduced the first languor into his ferocity? Emerging from the throng of the other living creatures, he has created a subtler confusion for himself; he has scrupulously exploited the ills of a life wrested from itself. Out of all he has undertaken to be healed of himself, a stranger disease has been constituted: his "civilization" is merely the effort to find remedies for an incurable—and coveted—state. The mind wilts at the approach of health: man is an invalid—or he is nothing. When, having thought of everything, he thinks of himself—for he manages this only by the detour of the universe, as if he were the last problem he proposes to himself—he remains astonished, confused, embarrassed. But he continues to prefer, to the nature which eternally capsizes into health, his own defeat.

(Since Adam men's entire effort has been to modify *man*. The aims of reform and of pedagogy, articulated at the expense of irreducible *data*, denature thought and distort its movement. Knowledge has no more desperate enemy than the educative instinct, at once optimistic and virulent, which no philosopher can escape: how would their systems be unscathed by it? Outside the Irremediable, everything is false; false this civilization which seeks to combat it, false the truths with which it arms itself.

Except for the ancient skeptics and the French moralists, it would be hard to cite a single mind whose theories, secretly or explicitly, do not tend to mold man. But he subsists unchanged, though he has followed the parade of noble precepts, proposed to his curiosity, offered to his ardor and to his uncertainty. Whereas all beings have their *place* in nature, man remains a metaphysically straying creature, lost in Life, a stranger to the Creation. No one has found a valid goal for history; but everyone has proposed one; and in the pullulation of goals so divergent and so fantastic, the notion of finality has been canceled out and vanishes into a mocking clause of the mind.

Each of us takes on himself that *unit of disaster* which is the phenomenon *man*. And the only meaning time has is to multiply these units, endlessly to enlarge these vertical sufferings which depend upon a nonentity of matter, upon the pride of a given name, and upon a solitude without appeal.)

The Key to Our Endurance

The man who managed, by an imagination overflowing with pity, to record all the sufferings, to be contemporary with all the pain and all the anguish of any given moment—such a man—supposing he could ever exist—would be a monster of love and the greatest victim in the history of the human heart. But it is futile to imagine such an impossibility. We need merely proceed to an investigation of ourselves, only undertake the archaeology of our alarms. If we venture into the torment of the days, it is because nothing halts this march except our pangs; those of others seem to us explicable and capable of being transcended: we believe they suffer because they lack sufficient will, courage, or lucidity. Each suffering, except ours, seems to us legitimate or absurdly intelligible; otherwise, mourning would be the unique constant in the versatility of our sentiments. But we wear only the mourning of ourselves. If we could understand and love the infinity of agonies which languish around us, all the lives which are hidden deaths, we should require as many hearts as there are suffering beings. And if we had a miraculously *present* memory which sustained the totality of our past pains, we should succumb beneath such a burden. *Life is possible only by the deficiencies of our imagination and our memory.*

We derive our power from our forgetting and from our incapacity to conceive of the plurality of simultaneous fates. No one could survive the instantaneous comprehension of universal grief, each heart being stirred only for a certain quantity of sufferings. There are something like material limits to our endurance; yet the expansion of each pang reaches and occasionally exceeds such limits: this is too often the source of our ruin. Whereupon the impression that each misery, each disappointment is infinite. Indeed they are, but only for us, for the limits of our own heart; and if the latter had the dimensions of space itself, our ills would be more spacious still, since every pain replaces the world, and for each unhappiness we require another universe. Reason vainly strives to show us the infinitesimal proportions of our disasters; it fails, confronted with our penchant for cosmogonic proliferation. Thus true madness is never due to chance or to the disasters of the brain, but to the false conception of space the heart creates for itself. . . .

Annihilation by Deliverance

A doctrine of salvation has meaning only if we start from the equation "existence equals suffering." It is neither a sudden realization, nor a series of reasonings which lead us to this equation, but the unconscious elaboration of our every moment, the contribution of all our experiences, minute or crucial. When we carry germs of disappointments and a kind of thirst to see them develop, the desire that the world should undermine our hopes at each step multiplies the voluptuous verifications of the disease. The arguments come later; the doctrine is constructed: there still remains only the danger of "wisdom." But, suppose we do not want to be free of suffering nor to conquer our contradictions and conflicts—what if we prefer the nuances of the incomplete and an affective dialectic to the *evenness* of a sublime impasse? Salvation ends everything; and ends us. Who, once *saved*, dares still call himself alive? We really live only by the refusal to be delivered from suffering and by a kind of religious temptation of irreligiosity. Salvation haunts only assassins and saints, those who have killed or transcended the creature; the rest wallow— dead drunk—in imperfection. . . .

The mistake of every doctrine of deliverance is to suppress

poetry, climate of the incomplete. The poet would betray himself if he aspired to be saved: salvation is the death of song, the negation of art and of the mind. How to feel integral with a conclusion? We can refine, we can farm our sufferings, but by what means can we free ourselves from them without *suspending ourselves*? Docile to malediction, we exist only insofar as we suffer. A soul enlarges and perishes only by as much *insupportable* as it assumes.

The Abstract Venom

Even our vague ills, our diffuse anxieties, degenerating into physiology, should by a converse impulse be restored to the maneuvers of the intelligence. If we raised ennui—tautological perception of the world, the dull ripple of duration—to the dignity of a deductive elegy, if we offered it the temptation of a glamorous sterility? Without resorting to an order superior to the soul, the soul collapses into the flesh—and physiology becomes the last word of our philosophic stupors. To transpose immediate poisons into intellectual currency, to make an instrument out of our palpable corruption, or else to mask the impurity of every sentiment and sensation by norms is a pursuit of elegance necessary to the mind, next to which the soul—that pathetic hyena—is merely profound and sinister. The mind *in itself* can be only *superficial*, its nature being uniquely concerned with the arrangement of conceptual events and not with their implications in the spheres they *signify*. Our states interest it only insofar as they are transposable. Thus melancholia emanates from our viscera and joins the cosmic void; but the mind adopts melancholia only filtered of what attaches it to the fragility of the senses; the mind *interprets* it; refined, melancholia becomes *point of view*: departmental melancholia. Theory lies in wait and seizes upon our venoms, and renders them less noxious. It is a degradation *from above,* the mind-as-amateur of pure intoxications—since it is the enemy of intensities.

The Consciousness of Misery

Everything conspires, elements and actions alike, to harm you. Arm yourself in disdain, isolate yourself in a fortress of disgust, dream of superhuman indifference? The echoes of time would persecute you in your ultimate absences. . . . When nothing can keep you from bleeding, ideas themselves turn red or encroach on each other like tumors. There is no specific in our pharmacies against existence; nothing but minor remedies for braggarts. But where is the antidote for lucid despair, perfectly articulated, proud, and sure? All of us are miserable, but how many know it? The consciousness of misery is too serious a disease to figure in an arithmetic of agonies or in the catalogues of the Incurable. It belittles the prestige of hell, and converts the slaughterhouses of time into idyls. What sin have you committed to be born, what crime to exist? Your suffering like your fate is without motive. To suffer, truly to suffer, is to accept the invasion of ills without the excuse of causality, as a favor of demented nature, as a negative miracle. . . .

In Time's sentence men take their place like commas, while, in order to end it, you have immobilized yourself into a period.

Interjective Thought

The idea of infinity must have been born on a day of slackening when some vague languor infiltrated into geometry, like the first act of knowledge at the moment when, in the silence of reflexes, a macabre shudder isolated the perception of its object. How many disgusts or nostalgias have we had to accumulate in order to waken at the end alone, tragically superior to the evidence! A forgotten sigh has made us take a step outside the immediate; a banal fatigue has alienated us from a landscape or a person; diffuse moans have separated us from sweet or timid innocences. The sum of these accidental distances constitutes—ledger of our days and nights—the gap which distinguishes us from the world, and which the mind strives to reduce and to restore to our fragile proportions. But the creation of each lassitude makes itself felt: where now to seek for the substance under our steps?

At first, it is in order to escape things that we think; then, when we have gone too far, in order to lose ourselves in the regret for our escape. . . . And so our concepts are linked together like dissimulated sighs, every reflection replaces an interjection, a plaintive tonality submerges the dignity of logic. Funereal hues dim our ideas, hints of the graveyard encumber our paragraphs: a whiff of mildew in our precepts, the last day of autumn in a timeless crystal. . . . The mind is defenseless against the miasmas which assail it, for they rise from the most corrupt place that exists between earth and heaven, from the place where madness lies down in tenderness, cloaca of utopias and den of dreams: our soul. And even then when we could change the laws of the universe or foresee its whims, our soul would subjugate us by its miseries, by the principle of its ruin. A soul which is not lost? Where is such a thing, so that we may draw up the interrogation, so that science, sanctity, and comedy may seize upon it!

Apotheosis of the Vague

We might apprehend the essence of nations—even more than that of individuals—by their way of participating in the *vague*. The specifics in which they live reveal only their transitory character, their peripheries, their appearances.

What a nation can express has only a historical value: its success in becoming; but what it cannot express, *its failure in the eternal*, is the unproductive thirst for itself: its effort to exhaust itself in expression being stricken with impotence, it fills the gap by certain words—allusions to the unspeakable. . . .

How many times, in our peregrinations outside the intellect, have we not rested our troubles in the shade of those *Sehnsuchts, yearnings, saudades*, those sonorous fruits grown for overripe hearts! Lift the veil from these words: do they conceal the same content? Is it possible that the same meaning lives and dies in the verbal ramifications of an identical stock? Is it conceivable that such diverse peoples experience nostalgia in the same way?

The man who struggles to find the formula for the *disease of the distant* becomes the victim of a rickety architecture. To get back to the source of these expressions of the vague, we must make an affective regression toward their essence, must drown in the ineffable and emerge from it with our concepts in tatters. Once our theoretical assurance and our pride in the intelligible is lost, we can try to understand everything, to understand everything *for itself*. Then we manage to rejoice in the inexpressible, to spend our days in the margin of the comprehensible, and to wallow in the suburbs of the sublime. In order to escape sterility, we must wear Reason's mourning. . . .

To live in expectation, in what is not yet, is to accept the stimulating disequilibrium implied by the very notion of *future*. Every nostalgia is a transcendence of the present. Even in the form of regret, it assumes a dynamic character: we want to force the past, we want to act retroactively, to protest against the irreversible. Life has a content only in the violation of time. The obsession of elsewhere is the impossibility of the moment; and this impossibility is nostalgia itself.

That the French should have refused to feel and above all to cultivate the imperfection of the indefinite is certainly suggestive. In a collective form, this disease does not exist in France: what the French call *cafard* has no metaphysical quality and ennui is managed singularly. The French repel all complacency toward the Possible; their language itself eliminates any complicity with its dangers. Is there any other nation which finds itself more at ease in the world, for which being *chez soi* has more meaning and more weight, for which immanence offers more attractions?

In order to desire something else *fundamentally*, we must be stripped of space and time, we must live in a minimum of relationship with a site, a moment. The reason the history of France offers so few discontinuities is that fidelity to its essence, which flatters our inclination to perfection and disappoints the craving for the incomplete which a tragic vision implies. The only contagious thing in

France is lucidity, the horror of being fooled, of being the victim of anything. This is why a Frenchman accepts a risk only when he is fully conscious of it; he *wants* to be fooled; he bandages his eyes; unconscious heroism rightly seems to him a lapse of taste, an inelegant sacrifice. But life's brutal ambiguity requires the triumph of the *impulse,* and not of the will, to be a corpse, to be metaphysically fooled.

If the French have burdened nostalgia with too much clarity, if they have stripped it of a certain intimate and dangerous glamor, *Sehnsucht,* on the other hand, exhausts whatever is insoluble about it in the conflicts of the German soul, torn between *Heimat* and Infinity.

How could it find satisfaction? On one side, the longing to be plunged into the undifferentiation of heart and hearth; on the other, to keep absorbing space in an unslaked desire. And since extent offers no limits, and since with it grows the penchant for new wanderings, the goal retreats according to the progress made. Whence the exotic taste, the passion for journeys, the delectation in landscape as landscape, the lack of inner form, the tortuous depth at once seductive and disheartening. There is no solution to the tension between *Heimat* and Infinity: for it is to be rooted and uprooted at one and the same time, and to have been unable to find a compromise between the fireside and the far-off. . . . Imperialism, deadly constant in its ultimate essence—what is it but the political and vulgarly concrete translation of *Sehnsucht?*

We cannot overemphasize the historical consequences of certain inner approximations. Now, nostalgia is one of these; it keeps us from resting in existence or in the absolute; it forces us to drift in the indistinct, to lose our foundations, to live *uncovered* in time.

To be torn from the earth, exiled in duration, cut off from one's immediate roots, is to long for a reintegration in the original sources dating from before the separation and the severance. Nostalgia is precisely to feel eternally distant from *chez soi*; and, outside the luminous proportions of Ennui, and outside of the contradictory postulation of *Heimat* and Infinity, it takes the form of the return to the finite, to the immediate, to a terrestrial and maternal appeal. Like the mind, the heart creates utopias: and of them all, the strangest is the utopia of a *natal* universe, where we rest from ourselves, a universe that is the cosmic pillow of all our lassitudes.

In nostalgic aspiration we do not want something palpable, but a kind of abstract warmth, heterogeneous to time and close to a paradisiac presentiment. Whatever does not accept existence as such borders on theology. Nostalgia is merely a sentimental theology, in which the Absolute is built with the elements of desire, in which God is Indeterminacy elaborated by languor.

Solitude—Schism of the Heart

We are doomed to perdition each time life does not reveal itself as a miracle, each time the moment no longer moans in a supernatural shudder. How renew that sensation of plenitude, those seconds of delirium, those volcanic flashes, those wonders of fervor which reduce God to an accident of our clay? By what subterfuge revive that explosion in which even music seems superficial, the castoff of our *inner organ*?

It is not in our power to remember the seizures which made us coincide with the start of movement, made us masters of the first moment of time and instantaneous artisans of the Creation. We perceive no more of Creation than its destitution, the grim reality: we live in order to unlearn ecstasy. And it is not the miracle which determines our tradition and our substance, but the void of a universe frustrated of its flames, engulfed in its own absences, exclusive object of our rumination: a lonely universe before a lonely heart, each predestined to disjoin and to exasperate each other in the antithesis. When the solitude is intensified to the point of constituting not so much our *datum* as our sole *faith*, we cease to be integral with the whole: heretics of existence, we are banished from the community of the living, whose sole virtue is to wait, gasping, for something which is not death. But we, emancipated from the fascination of such waiting, rejected from the ecumenicity of illusion—we are the most heretical sect of all, for our soul itself is born in heresy.

*

("When the soul is in a state of grace, its beauty is so high and so admirable that it far surpasses all that is beautiful in nature, and delights the eyes of God and the Angels"—Ignatius Loyola.

I have sought to settle in an ordinary grace; I have tried to liquidate all interrogations and vanish in an ignorant light, in any light disdainful of the intellect. But how attain to the sigh of felicity superior to problems, when no "beauty" illuminates you, and when God and the Angels are blind?

Once, when Teresa, patron saint of Spain and of your soul, prescribed a course of temptations and intoxications, the transcendent abyss amazed you like a fall into the heavens. But those heavens have vanished—like the temptations and intoxications—and in the cold heart the fevers of Avila are extinguished forever.

By what peculiarity of fate do certain beings, having reached the point where they might coincide with a faith, retreat to follow a path which leads them only to themselves—and hence nowhere? Is it out of fear that once installed in grace they might lose there their distinct virtues? Each man develops at the expense of his depths, each man is a mystic who denies himself: the earth is inhabited by various forms of grace *manqué*, by trampled mysteries.)

Twilight Thinkers

Athens was dying, and with it the worship of knowledge. The great systems had run their course: limited to the conceptual realm, they rejected the intervention of torments, the pursuit of deliverance and of inordinate meditation upon suffering. The declining city, having permitted the conversion of human disasters into theory, no matter what—sneeze or sudden death—was supplanting the old problems. The obsession with remedies marks the end of a civilization; the search for salvation, that of a philosophy. Plato and Aristotle had yielded to such preoccupations only for the sake of equilibrium; after them, such concerns prevailed in every domain.

Rome, waning, took from Athens only the echoes of its decadence and the reflections of its collapse. When the Greeks exercised their doubts throughout the Empire, the latter's downfall and that of philosophy were virtually consummated. All questions seeming legitimate, the superstition of formal limits no longer prevented the debauch of arbitrary curiosities. The infiltration of epicureanism and of stoicism was easy: ethics replaced the abstract structures, bastardized reason became the instrument of *praxis*. In the streets of Rome, with various recipes for "happiness," swarmed the epicureans and the stoics, experts in wisdom, noble charlatans appearing at the periphery of philosophy to treat an incurable and generalized lassitude. But their therapeutics lacked the mythology and the strange anecdotes which, in the universal enervation, were to constitute the vigor of a religion unconcerned with nuance, a religion originating more remotely than they. Wisdom is the last word of an expiring civilization, the nimbus of historic twilights, fatigue transfigured into a vision of the world, the last tolerance before the advent of other, newer gods—and of barbarism; wisdom, what we call *sagesse*, is also a vain attempt at melody among the environing death rattles. For the Sage—theoretician of a limpid death, hero of indifference, and symbol of the last stage of philosophy, of its degenerescence and its vacuity—has solved the problem of his own death . . . and has thereupon suppressed all problems. Provided with rarer absurdities, he is a limit-case, which we encounter in extreme periods as an exceptional confirmation of the general pathology.

Finding ourselves at a point symmetrical to the agony of the ancient world, a victim of the same sicknesses and under similarly ineluctable charms, we see the great systems destroyed by their limited perfection. For us too, everything becomes the substance of a philosophy without dignity and without rigor. . . . Thought's impersonal fate has been scattered into a thousand souls, a thousand humiliations of the Idea. . . . Not Leibnitz, Kant, or Hegel are of any help to us any longer. We have come with our own death to the doors of philosophy: rotting on their hinges, having nothing more to protect, they open of their own accord . . . and anything becomes a *philosophical subject*. Paragraphs are replaced by cries: the consequence is a philosophy of the *fundus animae*, whose intimacy will be reconnoitered in the appearances of history and the surfaces of time.

We too seek "happiness," either by frenzy or by disdain: to scorn it is not yet to forget it, and to reject it is a way of retaining it;

we too seek "salvation," if only by wanting nothing to do with it. And if we are the negative heroes of an overripe age, thereby we are its *contemporaries*: to betray one's age or to be its fervent adept expresses—in an apparent contradiction—one and the same act of participation. The lofty defeats, the subtle decrepitudes, the aspirations to timeless halos—all leading to wisdom—who would not recognize them in himself? Who does not feel the right to assert everything in the void around him, before the world vanishes in the dawn of an absolute or of a new negation? A god is always threatening on the horizon. We are in the margin of philosophy, since we consent to its end. Let us conduct ourselves so that the god does not settle in our thoughts, let us still keep our doubts, the appearances of equilibrium, and the temptation of immanent destiny, any arbitrary and fantastic aspiration being preferable to the inflexible truths. We change cures, finding none effective, none valid, because we have faith neither in the peace we seek nor in the pleasures we pursue. Versatile sages, we are the stoics and epicureans of modern Romes. . . .

Resources of Self-Destruction

Born in a prison, with burdens on our shoulders and our thoughts, we could not reach the end of a single day if the possibilities of ending it all did not incite us to begin the next day all over again. . . . Irons and the unbreathable air of this world strip us of everything, except the freedom to kill ourselves; and this freedom grants us a strength and a pride to triumph over the loads which overwhelm us.

What gift is more mysterious than being able to do what we will with ourselves and to refuse to do it? Consolation by a possible suicide widens into infinite space this realm where we are suffocating. The notion of destroying ourselves, the multiplicity of means for doing so, their ease and their proximity delight us and fill us with dread; for there is nothing simpler and more terrible than the action by which we decide irrevocably upon ourselves. In a single second we do away with all seconds; God himself could not do as much. But, braggart demons, we postpone our end: how could we renounce the display of our freedom, the show of our pride? . . .

The man who has never imagined his own annihilation, who has not anticipated recourse to the rope, the bullet, poison, or the sea, is a degraded galley slave or a worm crawling upon the cosmic carrion. This world can take everything from us, can forbid us everything, but no one has the power to keep us from wiping ourselves out. Every tool offers its help, every abyss invites us in; but all our instincts oppose the act. This contradiction develops an insoluble conflict in the mind. When we begin to reflect upon life, to discover in it an infinity of emptiness, our instincts have already turned themselves into guides and middlemen of our acts; they rein in the flight of our inspiration and the pliability of our detachment. If, at the moment of our birth, we were as conscious as we are at the end of adolescence, it is more than likely that at the age of five suicide would be a habitual phenomenon or even a question of honor. But we *wake* too late: we have against us the years nourished solely by the presence of the instincts, which can be only stupefied by the conclusions to which our meditations and our disappointments lead. And they react; yet, having acquired the consciousness of our freedom, we are masters of a resolve all the more tempting in that we do not take advantage of it. It makes us endure the days and, what is more, the nights; we are no longer poor, or crushed by adversity: we possess supreme resources. And even when we never exploit them, when we expire in the usual way, we have had a treasure in our very abandonments: what greater wealth than the suicide each of us bears within himself?

If the religions have forbidden us to die by our own hand, it is because they saw that such practices set an example of insubordination which humiliated temples and gods alike. The Council of Orleans regarded suicide as a sin more grievous than murder, for the murderer can always repent, be saved, whereas the man who has taken his own life has passed beyond the limits of salvation. But the act of suicide originates in a radical formula of salvation. Is not nothingness the equal of eternity? The solitary being has no need to declare war on the universe—he sends the ultimatum to himself. He no longer aspires *to be* forever, if in an incomparable action he has been *absolutely* himself. He rejects heaven and earth as he rejects himself. At least he will have achieved a plenitude of freedom inaccessible to the man who keeps looking for it in the future. . . .

No church, no civil institution has as yet invented a single argument valid against suicide. What answer is there to the man who can no longer endure life? No one is qualified to take another's burdens upon himself. And what power does dialectic have against the assault of irrefutable despairs and against a thousand unconsoled manifestations? Suicide is one of man's distinctive characteristics, one of his discoveries; no animal is capable of it, and the angels have scarcely guessed its existence; without it, human reality would be less curious, less picturesque: we should lack a strange climate and a series of deadly possibilities which have their aesthetic value, if only to introduce into tragedy certain new solutions and a variety of denouements.

The sages of antiquity, who put themselves to death as a proof of their maturity, had created a discipline of suicide which the moderns have unlearned. Doomed to an uninspired agony, we are neither authors of our extremities nor arbiters of our *adieux*; the end is no longer *our* end: we lack the excellence of a unique initiative— by which we might ransom an insipid and talentless life, as we lack the sublime cynicism, the ancient splendor of an art of dying. Habitués of despair, complacent corpses, we all outlive ourselves and die only to fulfill a futile formality. It is as if our life were attached to itself only to postpone the moment when we could get rid of it.

The Reactionary Angels

It is difficult to sit in judgment on the revolt of the least philosophical of the angels without a tinge of sympathy, amazement, and . . . blame. Injustice governs the universe. Everything which is done and undone there bears the stamp of a filthy fragility, as if matter were the fruit of a scandal at the core of nothingness. Each being feeds on the agony of some other; the moments rush like vampires upon time's anemia; the world is a receptacle of sobs. . . . In this slaughterhouse, to fold one's arms or to draw one's sword are equally vain gestures. No proud frenzy can shake space to its foundations or ennoble men's souls. Triumphs and failures follow one another according to an unknown law named *destiny*, a name to which we resort when, philosophically unprovided for, our sojourn here on earth or anywhere seems insoluble to us, a kind of curse to endure, senseless and undeserved. *Destiny*—favorite word in the vocabulary of the vanquished. . . . Greedy for a nomenclature of the Irremediable, we seek relief in verbal invention, in lights suspended over our disasters. Words are charitable: their frail reality deceives and consoles us. . . .

Thus "destiny," which can will nothing, is what has *willed* what happens to us. . . . Infatuated with the Irrational as the sole mode of explanation, we watch it tip the scale of our fate, which weighs only negative elements. Where find the pride to provoke the forces which have so decreed, and what is more, are not to be held responsible for this decree? Against whom wage the struggle, and where lead the assault when injustice haunts the air of our lungs, the space of our thoughts, the silence and the stupor of the stars? Our revolt is as ill conceived as the world which provokes it. How take it on ourselves to right wrongs when, like Don Quixote on his deathbed, we have lost—madness at its end, exhausted—vigor and illusion to confront the highroads, combats, and defeats? And how regain the energy of that seditious angel who, still at time's start, knew nothing of that pestilential wisdom in which our impulses asphyxiate? Where find enough verve and presumption to stigmatize the herd of the other angels, while here on earth to follow their colleague is to cast oneself still lower, while men's injustice imitates God's, and all rebellion sets the soul against infinity and breaks it there? The anonymous angels—huddled under their ageless wings, eternally victors and vanquished in God, numb to the deadly curiosities, dreamers parallel to the earthly griefs—who would dare to cast the first stone at them and, in defiance, divide their sleep? Revolt, the pride of downfall, takes its nobility only from its uselessness: sufferings awaken it and then abandon it; frenzy exalts it and disappointment denies it. . . . Revolt cannot have a meaning in a *non-valid* universe. . . .

*

(In this world nothing is in its place, beginning with this world itself. We must therefore not be surprised by the spectacle of human injustice. It is equally futile to refuse or to accept the social order: we must endure its changes for the better or the worse with a despairing conformism, as we endure birth, love, the weather, and death. Decomposition presides over the laws of life: closer to our dust than inanimate objects to theirs, we succumb before them and rush upon our destiny under the gaze of the apparently indestructible stars. But they themselves will crumble in a universe which only our heart takes seriously, later expiating its lack of irony by terrible lacerations. . . .

No one can correct God's injustice or that of men: every action is merely a special, apparently organized case of the original Chaos. We are swept on by a whirlwind which dates back to the dawn of time; and if this whirlwind has assumed the aspect of an order, it is only the better to do away with us. . . .)

The Concern for Decency

Under the goad of pain, the flesh awakens; lucid and lyrical substance, it sings its dissolution. So long as it was indistinguishable from nature, it rested in the oblivion of elements: the self had not yet seized upon it. Suffering matter frees itself from gravitation, no longer participates in the universe, isolates itself from the somnolent sum; for pain, an agent of separation, the active principle of individuation, denies the pleasures of a statistical destiny.

The truly solitary being is not the man who is abandoned by men, but the man who suffers in their midst, who drags his desert through the marketplace and deploys his talents as a smiling leper, a mountebank of the irreparable. The great solitaries were happy in the old days, knew nothing of duplicity, had nothing to hide: they conversed only with their own solitude. . . .

Of all the bonds which link us to things, there is not one which fails to slacken and dissolve under the influence of suffering, which frees us from everything except the obsession of ourselves and the sensation of being irrevocably *individual.* Suffering is solitude hypostatized as essence. By what means, then, communicate with others except by the prestidigitation of lying? For if we were not jugglers, if we had not learned the artifices of a knowing charlatanism, if indeed we were *sincere* to the point of shamelessness or tragedy—our underground worlds would vomit up oceans of gall, in which it would be a point of honor for us to vanish: thereby we should flee the unseemliness of so much grotesquerie and sublimity. At a certain degree of misery, all frankness becomes indecent. Job stopped just in time: one step further, and neither God nor his friends would have answered him again.

(One is "civilized" insofar as one does not proclaim one's leprosy, as one evinces respect for the elegant falsehoods forged by the ages. No one is entitled to stagger under the burden of his hours . . . every man harbors a possibility of apocalypse, but every man makes it a rule to level his own abysses. If each of us gave free rein to his solitude, God would have to remake the world, whose existence depends at every point on our education and on this fear we have of ourselves. . . . Chaos? Chaos is rejecting all you have learned, chaos is being *yourself*. . . .)

Gamut of the Void

I have seen one man pursue this goal, another that one; I have seen men fascinated by disparate objects, under the spell of dreams and plans at once vile and indefinable. Analyzing each case in isolation in order to penetrate the reasons for so much fervor squandered, I have realized the non-meaning of all action and all effort. Is there a single life which is not impregnated with life-giving errors, a single clear, transparent life without humiliating roots, without invented motives, without myths emerging from desires? Where is the action pure of all utility: sun abhorring incandescence, angel in a universe without faith, or idle worm in a world abandoned to immortality?

I have tried to protect myself against men, to react against their madness, to discern its source; I have listened and I have seen—and I have been afraid—afraid of acting for the same motives or for any motive whatever, of believing in the same ghosts or in any other ghost, of letting myself be engulfed by the same intoxications or by some other . . . afraid, in short, of raving in common and of expiring in a horde of ecstasies. I knew that by separating from someone, I was dispossessed of a fallacy, I was deprived of the illusion I was leaving him. . . . His feverish words revealed him the captive of an evidence absolute for him and absurd for me; on contact with his vacuity, I stripped myself of mine. . . . Whom can we adhere to without the feeling of deception—without blushing? We can justify only the man who practices, *in full awareness,* the irrational necessary to every action, and who embellishes with no dream the fiction to which he surrenders himself, as we can admire only a hero who dies without conviction, all the more ready for sacrifice in that he has seen through it. As for lovers, they would be hateful if among their grimaces the presentiment of death did not hover, caressing. . . . It is disturbing to think that we carry our secret—our illusion—into the grave, that we have not survived the mysterious mistake that vivified our every breath, that, except for the skeptics and whores among us, all founder in falsehood because they fail to divine the equivalence, in nullity, of triumphs and truths.

I wanted to suppress in myself the reasons men invoke in order to exist, in order to act. I wanted to become unspeakably normal—and here I am in dazed confusion, on a footing with fools, and as empty as they.

Certain Mornings

Regret not to be Atlas, not to be able to shrug my shoulders and watch the collapse of this laughable *matter.* . . . Rage takes the opposite path of cosmogony. By what mysteries do we wake, certain mornings, with the thirst to demolish the whole of creation, inert and animate alike? When the devil drowns himself in our veins, when our ideas turn convulsive and our desires cleave the light, the elements catch fire and consume themselves, while our fingers sift their ashes.

What nightmares have we sustained for nights on end to wake up in the mornings enemies of the sun? Must we liquidate ourselves to put an end to everything? What complicity, what bonds extend us into an intimacy with time? Life would be intolerable without the forces which deny it. Masters of a possible exit, of the *idea* of an escape, we might readily abolish ourselves and, at the apex of delirium, expectorate this universe.

. . . Or else pray and wait for other mornings.

(To write would be an insipid and superfluous action if we could weep at will, imitating women and children in their fits of rage. . . . In the substance of which we are made, in its deepest impurity, abides a principle of bitterness which only tears can sweeten. If, each time disappointments assail us, we had the possibility to be released from them by tears, all vague maladies and poetry itself would disappear. But a native reticence, aggravated by education, or a defective functioning of the lachrymal glands, dooms us to the martyrdom of dry eyes. And then shrieks, storms of swearing, self-maceration, and fingernails furrowing the flesh, with the consolations of a spectacle of blood, no longer figure among our therapeutic methods. It follows that we are all sick, and that each of us would require a Sahara in order to scream our lungs out, or the shores of a wild and elegiac sea in order to mingle with its fierce lamentations our even fiercer ones. Our paroxysms require the context of a parodic sublimity, of an apoplectic infinity, the vision of a hanging where the firmament would serve as a gallows to our carcasses and to the elements.)

Militant Mourning

All truths are against us. But we go on living, because we accept them in themselves, because we refuse to draw the consequences. Where is the man who has translated—in his behavior—a single conclusion of the lessons of astronomy, of biology, and who has decided never to leave his bed again out of rebellion or humility in the face of the sidereal distances or the natural phenomena? Has pride ever been conquered by the evidence of our unreality? And who was ever bold enough to do nothing because every action is senseless in infinity? The sciences prove our nothingness. But who has grasped their ultimate teaching? Who has become a hero of total sloth? No one folds his arms: we are busier than the ants and the bees. Yet if an ant, if a bee—by the miracle of an idea or by some temptation of singularity—were to isolate herself in the anthill or the hive, if she contemplated *from outside* the spectacle of her labors, would she still persist in her pains?

Only the rational animal has been able to learn nothing from his philosophy: he locates himself apart—and perseveres nonetheless in the same errors of effective appearance and void reality. Seen from outside, from any Archimedean point, life—with all its beliefs—is no longer possible, nor even conceivable. We can *act* only against the truth. Man starts over again every day, in spite of everything he knows, against everything he knows. He has extended this ambiguity to the point of vice: perspicacity is in mourning, but—strange contagion—this very mourning is active; thus we are led into a funeral procession to the Last Judgment; thus, out of the ultimate rest itself, out of history's final silence, we have made an activity: the staging of the agony, the need for dynamism even in the death-rattles. . . .

(The panting civilizations exhaust themselves faster than those that loll in eternity. China alone, thriving for millennia in the flower of her old age, offers an example to be followed; China alone long since arrived at a refined wisdom superior to philosophy: Taoism surpasses all the mind has conceived by way of detachment. We count by *generations*: it is the curse of scarcely century-old civilizations to have lost, in their rushed cadence, the atemporal consciousness.

By all evidence we are in the world to do nothing; but instead of nonchalantly promenading our corruption, we exude our sweat and grow winded upon the fetid air. All History is in a state of putrefaction; its odors shift toward the future: we rush toward it, if only for the fever inherent in any decomposition.

It is too late for humanity to be released from the illusion of *action*, it is especially too late for it to be raised to the *sanctity of sloth*.)

Immunity to Renunciation

Everything which deals with eternity inevitably turns into a commonplace. The world ends by accepting any revelation and resigns itself to any shudder, provided that a formula is found for it. The notion of universal futility—more dangerous than any scourge —has been debased into the obvious: everyone acknowledges as much, and no one behaves accordingly. The terror of an ultimate truth has been tamed; once it turns into a refrain, men no longer think about it, for they have learned by heart a thing which, merely glimpsed, should cast them into the abyss or salvation. The vision of Time's nullity has begotten saints and poets, and the despairs of a few solitaries, infatuated with anathema. . . .

This vision is no news to the crowd; the crowd continually asks: "what's the use?"; "what does it matter?"; "it's not the first time"; *"plus ça change . . ."*—and yet nothing happens, nothing intervenes: not one saint, not one poet more. . . . If the crowd conformed to a single one of these refrains, the face of the world would be transformed. But eternity—appearing from an anti-vital thought— cannot be a human reflex without danger for the performance of actions: it becomes a commonplace, so that we can forget it by a mechanical repetition. Sanctity is a risk like poetry. Men say "everything passes"—but how many grasp the bearing of this terrifying banality? How many flee life, celebrate or bewail it? Who is not imbued with the conviction that all is vanity? But who dares confront the consequences? The man with a metaphysical vocation is rarer than a monster—and yet each man contains the potential elements of this vocation. It was enough for one Hindu prince to see a cripple, an old man, and a corpse *to understand everything*; we see them and understand nothing, for nothing changes in our life. We cannot renounce anything; yet the evidences of vanity are in our reach. Invalids of hope, we are still waiting; and life is only the hypostatization of waiting. We wait for everything—even Nothingness—rather than be reduced to an eternal suspension, to a condition of neutral divinity, of a corpse. Thus the heart, which has made the Irreparable into an axiom, still hopes for surprises from it. Humanity lives in love with the events which deny it. . . .

The World's Equilibrium

The apparent symmetry of joys and pains has nothing to do with their equitable distribution: it results from the injustice which strikes certain individuals, thereby forcing them to compensate by their despondency for the others' unconcern. To endure the consequences of their actions, or to be saved from them—such is the lot of men. This discrimination is effected without any criterion: it is a fatality, an absurd apportionment, a fantastic selection. No one can elude the condemnation to happiness or misery, nor the innate sentence at the preposterous tribunal whose decision extends between the spermatozoon and the sepulcher.

Some men pay for all their joys, expiate all their pleasures, are accountable for all their intervals of oblivion: they will never be indebted for a single moment of happiness. For them a thousand acrimonies have crowned a shudder of pleasure as if they had no right to acknowledged contentments, as if their abandonment endangered the world's bestial equilibrium. . . . Were they happy in some landscape?—they will regret it in imminent disappointments; were they proud in their plans and their dreams? they will soon wake, as from a utopia, corrected by all-too-positive sufferings.

Thus there are sacrificed men who pay for the unconsciousness of others, who expiate not only their own happiness but that of strangers. Thus equilibrium is restored; the proportion of joys and pains becomes harmonious. If an obscure universal principle has decreed that you belong to the order of victims, you will end your days stamping underfoot the speck of paradise you hid within yourself, and whatever impulse gleamed in your eyes and your dreams will be sullied by the impurity of time, matter, and men. You will have a dungheap for pedestal, for tribune a rack and thumb-screw. You will be worthy of no more than a leprous glory and a crown of spit. Try to walk beside those entitled to everything, to whom all paths are open? But dust and ashes themselves will rise up to bar you from the exits of time and the evasions of dreams. Whatever direction you take, your steps will be mired, your voices will proclaim only the hymns of mud, and over your bent heads, your heavy hearts, in which only self-pity dwells, will pass no more than the breath of the happy, blessed toys of a nameless irony as little to blame as you are.

Farewell to Philosophy

I turned away from philosophy when it became impossible to discover in Kant any human weakness, any authentic accent of melancholy; in Kant and in all the philosophers. Compared to music, mysticism, and poetry, philosophical activity proceeds from a diminished impulse and a suspect depth, prestigious only for the timid and the tepid. Moreover, philosophy—impersonal anxiety, refuge among anemic ideas—is the recourse of all who would elude the corrupting exuberance of life. Almost all the philosophers came to a *good end*: that is the supreme argument against philosophy. Even Socrates' death has nothing tragic about it: it is a misunderstanding, the end of a pedagogue—and if Nietzsche foundered, it was as a poet and visionary: he expiated his ecstasies and not his arguments.

We cannot elude existence by explanations, we can only endure it, love or hate it, adore or dread it, in that alternation of happiness and horror which expresses the very rhythm of being, its oscillations, its dissonances, its bright or bitter vehemences.

Exposed by surprise or necessity to an irrefutable defeat, who does not raise his hands in prayer then, only to let them fall emptier still for the answers of philosophy? It would seem that its mission is to protect us as long as fate's neglect allows us to proceed on the brink of chaos, and to abandon us as soon as we are forced to plunge over the edge. And how could it be otherwise, when we see how little of humanity's suffering has passed into its philosophy? The philosophic exercise is not fruitful; it is merely honorable. We are always philosophers *with impunity*: a *métier* without fate which pours voluminous thoughts into our neutral and vacant hours, the hours refractory to the Old Testament, to Bach, and to Shakespeare. And have these thoughts materialized into a single page that is equivalent to one of Job's exclamations, of Macbeth's terrors, or the altitude of one of Bach's cantatas? We do not *argue* the universe; we *express* it. And philosophy does not express it. The real problems begin only after having ranged or exhausted it, after the last chapter of a huge tome which prints the final period as an abdication before the Unknown, in which all our moments are rooted and with which we must struggle because it is naturally more immediate, more important than our daily bread. Here the philosopher leaves us: enemy of disaster, he is sane as reason itself, and as prudent. And we remain in the company of an old plague victim, of a poet learned in every lunacy, and of a musician whose sublimity transcends the sphere of the heart. We begin to live authentically only where philosophy ends, at its wreck, when we have understood its terrible nullity, when we have understood that it was futile to resort to it, that it is *no help*.

(The great systems are actually no more than brilliant tautologies. What advantage is it to know that the nature of being consists in the "will to live," in "idea," or in the whim of God or of Chemistry? A mere proliferation of words, subtle displacements of meanings. What *is* loathes the verbal embrace, and our inmost experience reveals us nothing beyond the privileged and inexpressible moment. Moreover, Being itself is only a pretension of Nothingness.

We define only out of despair. We must have a formula, we must even have many, if only to give justification to the mind and a façade to the void.

Neither concept nor ecstasy are functional. When music plunges us into the "inwardness" of being, we rapidly return to the surface: the effects of the illusion scatter and our knowledge admits its nullity.

The things we touch and those we conceive are as improbable as our senses and our reason; we are *sure* only in our verbal universe, manageable at will—and ineffectual. Being is mute and the mind is garrulous. This is called *knowing*.

The philosophers' originality comes down to inventing terms. Since there are only three or four attitudes by which to confront the world—and about as many ways of dying—the nuances which multiply and diversify them derive from no more than the choice of words, bereft of any metaphysical range.

We are engulfed in a pleonastic universe, in which the questions and answers amount to the same thing.)

From Saint to Cynic

Mockery has degraded everything to the rank of a pretext, except for the Sun and Hope, except for the two conditions of life: the world's center and the heart's, the one dazzling, the other invisible. A skeleton, warming in the sun and hoping, would be more vigorous than a despairing Hercules weary of the light; a Being totally permeable to Hope would be more powerful than God and more vital than Life. Macbeth, "aweary of the sun," is the last of creatures, true death not being corruption but the disgust with our irradiation, the repulsion for all that is a seed, for all that grows in the warmth of illusion.

Man has profaned the things which are born and die under the sun, except for the sun; the things which are born and die in hope, except for hope. Not having had the courage to go further, he has imposed limits upon his cynicism. A cynic, who claims to be consistent, is a cynic in words only; his gestures make him the most contradictory being: no one can live after having decimated his superstitions. To reach total cynicism would require an effort which is the converse of sanctity's and at least as considerable; or else, imagine a saint who, having reached the pinnacle of his purification, discovers the vanity of the trouble he has taken—and the absurdity of God. . . .

Such a monster of lucidity would change the data of life: he would have the strength and the authority to question the very conditions of his existence; he would no longer be in danger of contradicting himself; no human failing would then weaken his audacities; having lost the religious respect we pay despite ourselves to our last illusions, he would make a plaything of his heart, and of the sun. . . .

Return to the Elements

If philosophy had made no progress since the pre-Socratics, there would be no reason to complain. Exhausted by the jumble of concepts, we end by realizing that our life is still lived out in the elements out of which they constituted the world, that it is the earth, fire, air, and water which condition us, that this rudimentary physics reveals the context of our ordeals and the principle of our torments. Having complicated these few elementary data, we have lost—fascinated by the decor and the structure of our theories—the understanding of Destiny, which nonetheless, unchanged, is the same as on the world's first day. Our existence reduced to its essence continues to be a struggle against the eternal elements, a struggle which our knowledge in no way alleviates. The heroes of every epoch are no less wretched than those of Homer, and if they have become *characters*, it is by losing vitality and greatness. How could the results of the sciences change man's metaphysical position? And what are the explorations of matter, the discoveries and the products of analysis beside the vedic hymns and those melancholies of historic dawn which crept into the world's anonymous poetry?

Since the most eloquent decadences edify us no further as to unhappiness than the stammerings of a shepherd, and ultimately there is more wisdom in the mockery of an idiot than in the investigations of the laboratories, is it not madness to pursue truth on the paths of time—or in books? Lao-tse, reduced to a few texts, is not more naïve than we who have read everything. Profundity is independent of knowledge. We translate to other levels the revelations of the ages, or we exploit original intuitions by the latest acquisitions of thought. Thus Hegel is a Heraclitus who has read Kant; and our Ennui is an affective Eleaticism, the fiction of diversity unmasked and exposed to the heart. . . .

Subterfuges

Only those who live outside of art draw the ultimate consequences. Suicide, sanctity, vice—so many forms of lack of talent. Direct or

disguised, confession by word, sound, or color halts the agglomera-
tion of inner forces and weakens them by projecting them back
toward the world outside. It is a salutary diminution which makes
every act of creation into a coefficient of escape. But the man who
accumulates energies lives under pressure, a slave to his own excesses;
nothing keeps him from foundering in the absolute. . . .

Authentic tragic existence is almost never to be found among
those who know how to manage the secret powers which exhaust
them; diminishing their soul by their work, where would they find
the energy to attain to the extremity of actions? A hero is fulfilled in
a proud modality of dying because he lacked the faculty of gradually
extinguishing himself in verse. All heroism expiates—by the genius
of the heart—a defaulting talent; every hero is a being without talent.
And it is this deficiency which projects him forward and enriches
him, while those who have by creation impoverished their inheritance of the unspeakable, are cast, as existences, into the background,
though their minds can be raised above all the rest.

A man eliminates himself from the rank of his kind by the
monastery or some other artifice—by morphine, masturbation, or
rum—whereas a form of expression might have saved him. But,
always present to himself, perfect possessor of his reserves and his
mistakes, bearing the sum of his life without the possibility of
diminishing it by the pretexts of art, invaded by self he can be only
total in his gestures and his resolutions, he can draw only a conclusion
affecting him *altogether*; he cannot relish the extremes; he is drowned
in them; and he actually drowns in vice, in God, or in his own blood,
whereas the cowardices of expression would have made him retreat
before the *supreme*. The man who *expresses himself* does not act
against himself; he knows only the *temptation* of ultimate consequences. And the deserter is not the man who draws them, but the
man who scatters and divulges himself for fear lest, surrendered to
himself, he will be ruined and wrecked.

Non-Resistance to Night

At first, we think we advance toward the light; then, wearied by an
aimless march, we lose our way: the earth, less and less secure, no

longer supports us; it opens under our feet. Vainly we should try to follow a path toward a sunlit goal; the shadows mount within and below us. No gleam to slow our descent: the abyss summons us, and we lend an ear. Above still remains all we wanted to be, all that has not had the power to raise us higher. And we, once in love with the peaks, then disappointed by them, we end by fondling our fall, we hurry to fulfill it, instruments of a strange execution, fascinated by the illusion of reaching the limits of the darkness, the frontiers of our nocturnal fate. Fear of the void transformed into a kind of voluptuous joy, what luck to gainsay the sun! Infinity in reverse, god that begins beneath our heels, ecstasy before the crevices of being, and thirst for a black halo, the Void is an inverted dream in which we are engulfed.

If delirium becomes our law, let us wear a subterranean nimbus, a crown in our fall. Dethroned from this world, let us carry its scepter in order to honor the night with a new splendor.

(And yet this fall—but for some moments of posturing—is far from being solemn and lyric. Habitually we sink into a nocturnal mud, into a darkness quite as mediocre as the light. . . . Life is merely a torpor in chiaroscuro, an inertia among the gleams and shadows, a caricature of that inward sun which makes us believe, illegitimately, in our eminence over the rest of matter. Nothing proves that we are more than nothing. In order to experience that continual expansion in which we rival the gods, in which our fevers triumph over our fears, we should have to remain at so high a temperature that it would finish us off in a few days. But our illuminations are instantaneous; falls are our rule. Life is what decomposes at every moment; it is a monotonous loss of light, an insipid dissolution in the darkness, without scepters, without halos. . . .)

Turning a Cold Shoulder to Time

Yesterday, today, tomorrow—these are servants' categories. For the idle man, sumptuously settled in the Inconsolable, and whom every moment torments, past, present, and future are merely variable appearances of one and the same disease, identical in its substance, inexorable in its insinuation, and monotonous in its persistence. And this disease is coextensive with Being—it is Being.

I was, I am, or I shall be—a question of grammar and not of existence. Fate—as a carnival of *chronos*—lends itself to conjugation, but, stripped of its masks, is revealed to be as motionless and naked as an epitaph. How can we grant more importance to the hour which is than to the one which was or which will be? The contempt in which servants live—and every man who adheres to time is a servant—represents a true state of grace, an enchanted obscuration; and this contempt—like a supernatural veil—covers the damnation to which every action engendered by desire is exposed. But for the disabused man of leisure, the pure fact of living, living pure of all *praxis*, is a task so wearying, that to endure existence as such seems to him an excessive occupation, an exhausting career—and every gesture inordinate, impracticable, and repealed.

Two-Faced Freedom

Though the problem of freedom is insoluble, we can always argue about it, always side with contingency or necessity. . . . Our temperaments and our prejudices facilitate an option which cuts short and simplifies the problem without solving it. Whereas no theoretical construction manages to make it apparent to us, to make us experience its dense and contradictory reality, a privileged intuition puts us at the very heart of freedom, despite all the arguments invented against it. And we are afraid; we are afraid of the enormity of the possible, not being prepared for a revelation so huge and so sudden, for that dangerous benefit to which we aspired and before which we retreat. What shall we do—accustomed to chains and laws—in the face of an infinity of initiatives, of a debauch of decisions? The seduction of the arbitrary alarms us. If we can begin any action, if there are no limits to inspiration and to our whims, how avoid our ruin in the intoxication of so much power?

Consciousness, shaken by this revelation, interrogates itself and trembles. Who, in a world where he can do anything, has not been dizzied? The murderer makes a limitless use of his freedom, and cannot resist the notion of his power. It is within the capacities of each one of us to take another's life. If all those we have killed in thought were to disappear for good, the earth would be depopulated. We bear within us a reticent executioner, an unrealized criminal. And those who lack the boldness to acknowledge their homicidal tendencies, murder in dreams, people their nightmares with corpses. Before an absolute tribunal, only the angels would be acquitted. For there has never been a human being who has not—at least unconsciously—desired the death of another human being. Each of us drags after him a cemetery of friends and enemies; and it matters little whether this graveyard is relegated to the heart's abyss or projected to the surface of our desires.

Freedom, conceived in its ultimate implications, raises the question of our life or of others' lives; it involves the dual possibility of saving or destroying us. But we feel free, we understand our opportunities and our dangers only by fits and starts. And it is the intermittence of these fits and starts, their rarity, which explains why this world is no more than a mediocre slaughterhouse and a fictive paradise. To argue about freedom leads to no consequence in good or evil; but we have only moments to realize that *everything* depends on us. . . . Freedom is an *ethical* principle of *demonic* essence.

Overworked by Dreams

If we could conserve the energy we lavish in that series of dreams we nightly leave behind us, the mind's depth and subtlety would reach unimaginable proportions. The scaffolding of a nightmare requires a nervous expenditure more exhausting than the best articulated theoretical construction. How, after waking, begin again the task of aligning ideas when, in our unconscious, we were mixed up with grotesque and marvelous spectacles, we were sailing among the spheres without the shackles of anti-poetic Causality? For hours we were like drunken gods—and suddenly, our open eyes erasing night's infinity, we must resume, in day's mediocrity, the enterprise of insipid problems, without any of the night's hallucinations to help us. The glorious and deadly fantasy was all for nothing then; sleep has exhausted us in vain. Waking, another kind of weariness awaits us; after having had just time enough to forget the night's, we are at grips with the dawn's. We have labored hours and hours in horizontal immobility without our brain's deriving the least advantage of its absurd activity. An imbecile who was not victimized by this waste, who might accumulate all his resources without dissipating them in dreams, would be able—owner of an ideal state of waking—to disentangle all the snags of the metaphysical lies or initiate himself into the most inextricable difficulties of mathematics.

After each night we are emptier: our mysteries and our griefs have leaked away into our dreams. Thus sleep's labor not only diminishes the power of our thought, but even that of our secrets. . . .

The Model Traitor

Since life can be fulfilled only within individuation—that last bastion of solitude—each being is necessary alone by the fact that he is an individual. Yet all individuals are not alone in the same way nor with the same intensity: each occupies a different rank in the hierarchy of solitude; at one extreme stands the traitor: he is an individual to the point of exasperation. In this sense, Judas is the loneliest being in the history of Christianity, but not in the history of solitude. He betrayed only a god; he *knew* what he betrayed; he betrayed *someone*, as so many others betray *something*: a country or other more or less collective pretexts. The betrayal which focuses on a specific object, even if it involves dishonor or death, is not at all mysterious: we always have the image of what we want to destroy; guilt is clear, whether admitted or denied. The others cast you out, and you resign yourself to the cell or the guillotine. . . .

But there exists a much more complex modality of betrayal, without immediate reference, without relation to an object or a person. Thus: to abandon *everything* without knowing what this everything represents; to isolate yourself from your *milieu*; to reject—by a metaphysical divorce—the substance which has molded you, which surrounds you, and which carries you.

Who, and by what defiance, can challenge existence with impunity? Who, and by what efforts, can achieve a liquidation of the very principle of his own breath? Yet the will to undermine the foundations of all that exists produces a craving for negative effectiveness, powerful and ineffable as a whiff of remorse corrupting the young vitality of a hope. . . .

When you have betrayed *being* you bear with you only a vague discomfort; there is no image sustaining the object which provokes the sensation of infamy. No one casts the first stone; you are a respectable citizen as before; you enjoy the honors of the city, the consideration of your kind; the laws protect you; you are as estimable as anyone else—and yet no one sees that you are living your funeral in advance and that your death can add nothing to your irremediably established condition. This is because the traitor to existence is accountable only to himself. Who else can ask him for an accounting? If you denounce neither a man nor an institution, you run no risk; no law protects Reality, but all of them punish you for the merest prejudice against its appearances. You are entitled to sap Being itself, but no human being; you may legally demolish the foundations of all that *is*, but prison or death awaits your least infringement of individual powers. Nothing protects Existence: there is no case against metaphysical traitors, against the Buddhas who reject salvation, for we judge them traitors only to their own lives. Yet of all malefactors, these are the most harmful: they do not attack the fruit, but the very sap of the universe. Their punishment? They alone know what it is. . . .

It may be that in every traitor there is a thirst for opprobrium, and that his choice of betrayal depends on the degree of solitude he aspires to. Who has not experienced the desire to perpetrate an incomparable crime which would exclude him from the human race? Who has not coveted ignominy in order to sever for good the links which attach him to others, to suffer a condemnation without appeal and thereby to reach the peace of the abyss? And when we break with the universe, is it not for the calm of an unpardonable crime? A

Judas with the soul of a Buddha—what a model for a coming and concluding humanity!

In One of the Earth's Attics

"I have dreamed of distant springs, of a sun shining on nothing but seafoam and the oblivion of my birth, of a sun opposed to the earth and to this disease of finding nothing anywhere but the desire to be somewhere else. The earthly fate—who has inflicted it upon us, who has chained us to this morose matter, a petrified tear against which—born of time—our tears shatter, whereas it has fallen, immemorial, from God's first shudder?

"I have loathed the planet's noons and midnights, I have longed for a world without weather, without hours and the fear that swells them, I have hated the sighs of mortals under the weight of ages. Where is the moment without end and without desire, and that primal vacancy insensitive to the presentiments of disaster and of life? I have sought for the geography of Nothingness, of unknown seas and another sun—pure of the scandal of life-bearing rays—I have sought for the rocking of a skeptical ocean in which islands and axioms are drowned, the vast liquid narcotic, tepid and sweet and tired of knowledge. . . .

"This earth—sin of the Creator! But I no longer want to expiate others' sins. I want to be cured of my begetting in an agony outside the continents, in some fluid desert, in an impersonal shipwreck."

Indefinite Horror

It is not the outbreak of a specific evil which reminds us of our fragility: there are vaguer but more troublesome warnings to signify our imminent excommunication from the temporal. The approach of disgust, of that sensation which physiologically separates us from the world, shows how destructible is the solidity of our instincts or the consistency of our attachments. In health, our flesh echoes the universal pulsation and our blood reproduces its cadence; in disgust, which lies in wait for us like a potential hell in order to suddenly seize upon us afterwards, we are as isolated in the whole as a monster imagined by some teratology of solitude.

The critical point of our vitality is not disease—which is struggle—but that indefinite horror which rejects everything and strips our desires of the power to procreate new mistakes. The senses lose their sap, the veins dry up, and the organs no longer perceive anything but the interval separating them from their own functions. Everything turns insipid: provender and dreams. No more aroma in matter and no more enigma in meditation; gastronomy and meta-physics both become victims of our want of appetite. We spend hours waiting for other hours, waiting for the moments which no longer flee time, the faithful moments which reinstate us in the mediocrity of health . . . and the amnesia of its dangers.

(Greed for space, unconscious covetousness of the future, health shows us how *superficial* the level of life is as such, and how incompatible organic equilibrium is with inner depth.

The mind, in its range, proceeds from our compromised functions: it takes wing insofar as the void dilates within our organs. We are *healthy* only insofar as we are not specifically ourselves: it is our disgusts which individualize us; our melancholies which grant us a name; our losses which make us possessors of our . . . self. We are ourselves only by the sum of our failures.)

Unconscious Dogmas

We are in a position to penetrate someone's *mistake*, to show him the inanity of his plans and intentions; but how wrest him from his persistence in time, when he conceals a fanaticism as inveterate as his instincts, as old as his prejudices? We bear within us—like an unchallengeable treasure—an amalgam of unworthy beliefs and certitudes. And even the man who manages to rid himself of them, to vanquish them, remains—in the desert of his lucidity—a fanatic still: a fanatic of himself, of his own existence; he has scoured all his obsessions, except for the terrain where they flourish; he has lost all his fixed points, except for the fixity from which they proceed. Life has dogmas more immutable than theology, each existence being anchored in infallibilities which exceed all the lucubrations of madness or of faith. Even the skeptic, in love with his doubts, turns out to be a fanatic of skepticism. Man is the dogmatic being *par excellence*; and his dogmas are all the deeper when he does not formulate them, when he is unaware of them, and when he follows them.

We all believe in many more things than we think, we harbor intolerances, we cherish bloody prejudices, and, defending our ideas with extreme means, we travel the world like ambulatory and irrefragable fortresses. Each of us is a supreme dogma to himself; no theology protects its god as we protect our self; and if we assail this self with doubts and call it into question, we do so only by a pseudo-elegance of our pride: the case is already won.

How escape the absolute of oneself? One would have to imagine a being without instincts, without a name, and to whom his own image would be unknown. But everything in the world gives us back our own features; night itself is never dark enough to keep us from being reflected in it. Too present to ourselves, our non-existence before birth and after death influences us only as a notion and only for a few moments; we experience the fever of our duration as an eternity which falters but which nonetheless remains unexhaustible in its principle.

The man who does not adore himself is yet to be born. Everything that lives loves itself; if not, what would be the source of the dread which breaks out in the depths and on the surfaces of life? Each of us is, for himself, the one fixed point in the universe. And if someone dies for an idea, it is because it is *his* idea, and his idea is *his life*.

No critique of any kind of reason will waken man from his "dogmatic sleep." It may shake the unconscious certitudes which abound in his philosophy and substitute more flexible propositions for his rigid affirmations, but how, by a rational procedure, will it manage to shake the creature, huddled over its own dogmas, without bringing about its very death?

Duality

There is a vulgarity which makes us admit anything in this world, but which is not powerful enough to make us admit this world itself. Hence we can endure life's miseries even as we repudiate Life, let ourselves be swept away by the frenzies of desire even as we reject Desire. In the assent to existence there is a kind of baseness, which we escape by means of our prides and our regrets, but particularly by means of the melancholy which keeps us from sliding into a final affirmation, wrested from our cowardice. Is anything viler than to say *yes* to the world? And yet we keep multiplying that consent, that trivial repetition, that loyalty oath to life, denied only by everything in us that rejects vulgarity.

We can live the way the others do and yet conceal a *"no"* greater than the world: that is melancholy's infinity. . . .

(We can love only the beings who do not exceed the minimum of vulgarity indispensable for life itself. Yet it would be difficult to delimit the quantity of such vulgarity, especially since no action can do without it. All of life's rejects prove that they were insufficiently sordid. . . . The man who prevails in the conflict with his neighbors stands on top of a dungheap; and the man who is vanquished there pays for a purity he has been unwilling to sully. In every man, nothing is more alive and true than his own vulgarity, source of all that is vital in elemental terms. But, on the other hand, the more deeply rooted you are in life, the more contemptible you are. The man who does not spread a vague funereal radiation around himself, and who in passing fails to leave a whiff of melancholy from remote worlds—that man belongs to sub-zoology, more specifically to human history.

The opposition between vulgarity and melancholy is so irreducible that next to it all other oppositions seem to be inventions of the mind, arbitrary and entertaining; even the most decisive antimonies blur beside this opposition in which are brought face to face—according to a predestined dosage—our lower depths and our dreaming gall.)

The Renegade

He remembers being born somewhere, having believed in native errors, having proposed principles and preached inflammatory stupidities. He blushes for it . . . and strives to abjure his past, his real or imaginary fatherlands, the truths generated in his very marrow. He will find peace only after having annihilated in himself the last reflex of the citizen, the last inherited enthusiasm. How could the heart's habits still chain him, when he seeks liberation from genealogies and when even the ideal of the ancient sage, scorner of all cities, seems to him a compromise? The man who can no longer take sides because all men are necessarily right and wrong, because everything is at once justified and irrational—that man must renounce his own name, tread his identity underfoot, and begin a new life in impassibility or despair. Or otherwise, invent another genre of solitude, expatriate himself in the void, and pursue—by means of one exile or another—the stages of uprootedness. Released from all prejudices, he becomes the unusable man *par excellence*, to whom no one turns and whom no one fears because he admits and repudiates everything with the same detachment. Less dangerous than a heedless insect, he is nonetheless a scourge for Life, for it has vanished from his vocabulary, with the seven days of the Creation. And Life would forgive him, if at least he relished Chaos, which is where Life began. But he denies the feverish origins, beginning with his own, and preserves, with regard to the world, only a cold memory, a polite regret.

(From denial to denial, his existence is diminished: vaguer and more unreal than a syllogism of sighs, how could he still be a creature of flesh and blood? Anemic, he rivals the Idea itself; he has abstracted himself from his ancestors, from his friends, from every soul and himself; in his veins, once turbulent, rests a light from another world. Liberated from what he *has* lived, unconcerned by what he *will* live, he demolishes the signposts on all his roads, and wrests himself from the dials of all time. "I shall never meet myself again," he decides, happy to turn his last hatred against himself, happier still to annihilate—*in his forgiveness*—all beings, all things.)

Shades of the Future

We are justified in imagining a time when we shall have transcended everything, even music, even poetry, a time when, detractors of our traditions and our transports, we shall achieve such a disavowal of ourselves that, weary of a known grave, we shall make our way through the days in a threadbare shroud. When a sonnet, whose rigor raises the verbal world above a splendidly imagined cosmos—when a sonnet ceases to be a temptation for our tears, and when in the middle of a sonata our yawns win out over our emotion, then the graveyards will have nothing more to do with us, for they receive only fresh corpses, still imbued with a suspicion of warmth and a memory of life.

Before our old age a time will come when, retracing our ardors, and bent beneath the recantations of the flesh, we shall walk, half-carrion, half-specter. . . . We shall have repressed—out of fear of complicity with illusion—any palpitation within us. Unable to have disembodied our life in a sonnet, we shall drag our corruption in shreds and tatters, and for having outstripped music and death alike, we shall stumble, blind, toward a funereal immortality. . . .

The Flower of Fixed Ideas

So long as man is protected by madness, he functions and flourishes; but when he frees himself from the fruitful tyranny of fixed ideas, he is lost, ruined. He begins to accept everything, to wrap not only minor abuses in his tolerance, but crimes and monstrosities, vices and aberrations: everything is worth the same to him. His indulgence, self-destroying as it is, extends to all the guilty, to the victims and the executioners; he takes all sides, because he espouses all opinions; gelatinous, contaminated by infinity, he has lost his "character," lacking any point of reference, any obsession. The universal view melts things into a blur, and the man who still makes them out, being neither their friend nor their enemy, bears in himself a wax heart which indiscriminately takes the form of objects and beings. His pity is addressed to . . . existence, and his charity is that of doubt and not that of love; a skeptical charity, consequence of knowledge, which excuses all anomalies. But the man who takes sides, who lives in the folly of decision and choice, is never charitable; incapable of comprehending all points of view, confined in the horizon of his desires and his principles, he plunges into a *hypnosis of the finite*. This is because creatures flourish only by turning their backs on the universal. . . . To be something—unconditional—is always a form of madness from which life—flower of fixed idea—frees itself only to fade.

The "Celestial Dog"

Unknowable, what a man must lose to have the courage to confront the conventions—unknowable what Diogenes lost to become the man who permitted himself everything, who translated his innermost thoughts into actions with a supernatural insolence, like some libidinous yet pure god of knowledge. No one was so frank; a limit case of sincerity and lucidity as well as an example of what we could be if education and hypocrisy did not rein in our desires and our gestures.

"One day a man invited him into a richly furnished house, saying 'be careful not to spit on the floor.' Diogenes, who needed to spit, spat in his face, exclaiming that it was the only dirty place he could find where spitting was permitted."—Diogenes Laërtius.

Who, after being received by a rich man, has not longed oceans of saliva to expectorate on all the owners of the earth? And who has not swallowed his own spittle for fear of casting it in the face of some stout and respected thief?

We are all absurdly prudent and timid: cynicism is not something we are taught in school. Nor is pride.

"Menippus, in his work entitled *The Virtue of Diogenes*, tells how he was captured and sold as a slave, and that he was asked what he knew how to do. Diogenes answered: 'Command!' and shouted to the herald: 'Ask who wants to buy a master.'"

The man who affronted Alexander and Plato, who masturbated in the marketplace ("If only heaven let us rub our bellies too, and that be enough to stave off hunger!"), the man of the famous cask and the famous lantern, and who in his youth was a counterfeiter (what higher dignity for a cynic?), what must his experience have been of his neighbors? Certainly our own, yet with this difference: that man was the sole substance of his reflection and his contempt. Without suffering the falsifications of any ethic and any metaphysic, he strove to strip man in order to show him to us nakeder and more abominable than any comedy, any apocalypse has done.

"Socrates gone mad," Plato called him—*Socrates turned sincere* is what he should have said, Socrates renouncing the Good, abjuring formulas and the City, Socrates turning, finally, into a psychologist and nothing more. But Socrates—even sublime—remains conventional; he remains a *master*, an *edifying* model. Only Diogenes proposes nothing; the basis of his attitude—and of cynicism in its essence—is determined by a testicular horror of the absurdity of being man.

The thinker who reflects without illusion upon human reality, if he wants to remain within the world, and if he eliminates mysticism as an escape-hatch, ends up with a vision in which are mingled wisdom, bitterness, and farce; and if he chooses the marketplace as the site of his solitude, he musters his verve in mocking his "kind" or in exhibiting his disgust, a disgust which today, with Christianity and the police, we can no longer permit ourselves. Two thousand years of oaths and codes have sweetened our bile; moreover, in a hurried world, who would stop to answer our insolences, to delight in our howls?

That the greatest connoisseur of human beings should have been nicknamd "dog" proves that man has never had the courage to accept his authentic image and that he has always rejected truths without accommodations. Diogenes suppressed *pose* in himself. What a monster in other men's eyes! To have an honorable place in philosophy you must be an actor, you must respect the play of ideas and exercise yourself over false problems. In no case must man as such be your *business*. Again, according to Diogenes Laërtius: "At the Olympic games, when the herald proclaimed: 'Dioxippus has vanquished men!' Diogenes answered: 'He has vanquished only slaves—men are my business.'" And indeed he vanquished men as no one else has ever done, with weapons more dreadful than those of conquerors, though he owned only a broom, the least proprietary of all beggars, true saint of mockery.

By a lucky accident, he was born before the Cross made its appearance. Who knows if, grafted on his detachment, some unhealthy temptation of extra-human risk might not have induced him to become an ordinary ascetic, later canonized, lost in the mass of the blessed and the maze of the calendar? Then he would have gone mad, he too, the most profoundly normal of men, since he was remote from all teaching and all doctrine. The hideous countenance of man—Diogenes was the only one to reveal that to us. The merits of cynicism have been dimmed and downtrodden by a religion opposed to the evident. But the moment has come to confront the truths of the Son of God with those of this "celestial dog," as a poet of his time called him.

Ambiguity of Genius

All inspiration proceeds from a faculty of exaggeration: lyricism— and the whole world of metaphor—would be a pitiable excitation without that rapture which dilates words until they burst. When the elements or the dimensions of the cosmos seem too diminished to serve as terms of comparison for our conditions, poetry needs—in order to transcend its stage of virtuality and imminence—only a little clarity in the flashes which prefigure and beget it. No true inspiration fails to rise out of the anomaly of a soul vaster than the world. . . . In the verbal conflagration of a Shakespeare and a Shelley we smell the ash of words, backwash and effluvium of an impossible cosmogony. The terms encroach upon each other, as though none could attain the equivalent of the inner dilation; this is the hernia of the image, the transcendent rupture of poor words, born of everyday use and miraculously raised to the heart's altitudes. The truths of beauty are fed on exaggerations which, upon the merest analysis, turn out to be monstrous and meaningless. Poetry: demiurgical divagation of the vocabulary. . . . Has charlatanism ever been more effectively combined with ecstasy? Lying, the wellspring of all tears! such is the imposture of genius and the secret of art. Trifles swollen to the heavens; the improbable, generator of a universe! In every genius coexists a braggart and a god.

Idolatry of Disaster

All that we build beyond raw existence, all the many powers which give the world a physiognomy, we owe to Misfortune—architect of diversity, intelligible instrument of our actions. What its sphere fails to engross transcends us: what meaning could an event have which fails to be overwhelming? The Future *awaits* us in order to immolate us: the mind records nothing but the fracture of existence now, and the senses still vibrate only in the expectation of disaster. . . . How avoid considering the fate of Chateaubriand's sister Lucile, or of Karoline von Günderode, and murmuring with the former: "I shall fall into the sleep of death upon my destiny," or gulping the latter's despair which plunged a dagger into her heart? Apart from a few examples of exhaustive melancholy, and a few unequaled suicides, men are merely puppets stuffed with red globules in order to beget history and its grimaces.

When, idolaters of disaster, we make it the agent and the substance of Becoming, we bathe in the limpidity of the prescribed fate, in a dawn of catastrophes, in a fruitful Gehenna. . . . But when, imagining we have exhausted it, we fear we shall outlive it, existence darkens and no longer *becomes*. And we dread readapting ourselves to Hope . . . betraying our disaster, betraying ourselves. . . .

The Demon

He is there, in the blood's inferno, in the bitterness of each cell, in the shudder of our nerves, in those contrary prayers exhaled by hate, everywhere where he makes, out of horror, his comfort. Should I let him undermine my hours, when as a meticulous accomplice of my destruction I could vomit up my hopes and desist from myself? He shares—murderous tenant—my bed, my oblivions, and my insomnias; to lose him, my own loss is necessary. And when you have only a body and a soul, the one too heavy and the other too dim, how bear as well an additional weight, a further darkness? How drag your way through a dark time? I dream of a golden moment outside of Becoming, a sunlit moment transcending the torment of the organs and the melody of their decomposition.

To hear the sobs—agonized, joyous—of that Evil One who wriggles through your thoughts, and not to strangle the intruder? But if you attack him, it will only be out of some futile self-indulgence. He is already your pseudonym; you cannot do him violence without impunity. Why evade the approach of the last act? Why not attack yourself in your own name?

(It would be quite false to suppose that the demoniac "revelation" is a presence inseparable from our duration; yet when we are gripped by it, we cannot imagine the quantity of neutral moments we have lived through *before*. To invoke the *devil* is to tinge with a vestige of theology an ambiguous excitation which our pride refuses to accept as such. But who does not know these fears, in which we find ourselves face to face with the Prince of Darkness? Our pride needs a name, a great name in order to baptize an anguish which would be pitiable if it emanated only from physiology. The traditional explanation seems more flattering to us; a residue of metaphysics suits the mind. . . .

It is in this way that—in order to veil our too immediate ills—we resort to elegant, although obsolete, entities. How admit that our most mysterious deliriums proceed from no more than nervous diseases, whereas it is enough for us to think of the Demon in us or outside us in order to stand up straight again at once? We inherit from our ancestors that propensity to objectivize our inmost evils; mythology has impregnated our blood and literature has sustained in us a relish for *effects*. . . .)

The Mockery of a "New Life"

Nailed to ourselves, we lack the capacity of leaving the path inscribed in the innateness of our despair. Exempt ourselves from life because it is not our element? No one hands out diplomas of non-existence. We must persevere in breathing, feel the air burn our lips, accumulate regrets at the heart of a reality which we have not hoped for, and renounce giving an explanation for the Disease which brings about our downfall. When each moment of time rushes upon us like a dagger, when our flesh, instigated by our desires, refuses to be petrified—how confront a single moment added to our fate? With the help of what artifices might we find the strength of illusion to go in search of another life—a new life?

It is because all men who cast a glance over their past ruins imagine—in order to avoid the ruins to come—that it is in their power to recommence something radically new. They make themselves a solemn promise, waiting for a miracle which would extricate them from this average abyss into which fate has plunged them. But nothing happens. They all continue to be the same, modified only by the accentuation of this tendency to decline which is their characteristic. We see around us only dilapidated inspirations and ardors: every man *promises* everything, but every man lives to know the fragility of his spark and Life's lack of genius in his life. The authenticity of an existence consists in its own ruin. The crown of our Becoming: a path that looks glorious and which leads to a rout; the garland of our gifts: camouflage of our gangrene. . . . Under the sun triumphs a carrion spring; beauty itself is merely death preening among the buds. . . .

I have known no "new" life which was not illusory and compromised at its roots. I have seen each man advance into time to be isolated in an anguished rumination and to fall back into himself with, as the sign of renewal, the unforeseen grimace of his own hopes.

Triple Impasse

The mind discovers Identity; the soul, Ennui; the body, Sloth. It is one and the same principle of invariability, differently expressed under the three forms of the universal yawn.

The monotony of existence justifies the rationalists' thesis; it shows us a legal universe in which everything is anticipated and adjusted; the barbarism of no surprise comes to trouble its harmony.

If the same mind discovers Contradiction, the same soul, Delirium, the same body, Frenzy, it is in order to beget new unrealities, to escape a universe too demonstrably the same; and it is the anti-rationalists' thesis which prevails. The flowering of absurdities reveals an existence before which all clarity of vision seems mockingly poor. This is the perpetual aggression of the Unforeseeable.

Between these two tendencies, man wields his ambiguity: finding his *place* in neither life nor Idea, he supposes himself predestined to the Arbitrary; yet his intoxication of freedom is only a shudder within a fatality, the form of his fate being no less regulated than that of a sonnet or a star.

Cosmogony of Desire

Having lived out—having *verified* all the arguments against life—I have stripped it of its savors, and wallowing in its lees, I have experienced its nakedness. I have known post-sexual metaphysics, the void of the futilely procreated universe, and that dissipation of sweat which plunges you into an age-old chill, anterior to the rages of matter. And I have tried to be faithful to my knowledge, to force my instincts to yield, and realized that it is no use wielding the weapons of nothingness if you cannot turn them against yourself. For the outburst of desires, amid our knowledge which contradicts them, creates a dreadful conflict between our mind opposing the Creation and the irrational substratum which binds us to it still.

Each desire humiliates the sum of our truths and forces us to reconsider our negations. We endure a practical defeat; yet our principles remain unshakable. . . . We hoped to be no longer children of this world, and here we are subject to the appetites like equivocal ascetics, masters of time and grafted to our glands. But this interplay is limitless: each of our desires recreates the world and each of our thoughts annihilates it. . . . In everyday life, cosmogony alternates with apocalypse: quotidian creators and wreckers, we enact on an infinitesimal scale the eternal myths, and each of our moments reproduces and prefigures the fate of seed and cinder pertaining to Infinity.

Interpretation of Actions

No one would perform the merest action without the feeling that this action is the one and only reality. Such blindness is the absolute basis, the indisputable principle, of all that exists. The man who *argues* merely proves that he *is* less, that doubt has sapped his vitality. . . . But amid his very doubts, he must feel the *importance* of his progress toward negation. To know that *nothing is worth the trouble* becomes implicitly a belief, hence a possibility of *action*; this is because even a trifle of existence presupposes an unavowed faith; a simple step—even toward a mock-up of reality—is an apostasy with regard to nothingness; breathing itself proceeds from an implicit fanaticism, like any participation in movement. . . .

Life without Objective

Neutral ideas like dry eyes; dull looks which strip things of all dimension; self-auscultations which reduce the feelings to phenomena of attention; a vaporous life, without tears and without laughter—how to inculcate a sap, a vernal vulgarity? And how to endure this resigning heart, this time too blunted to transmit even to its own seasons the ferment of growth and dissolution?

When you have seen a corruption in every conviction and in every attachment a profanation, you no longer have the right to expect, on earth or elsewhere, a fate modified by hope. You must choose some ideal, absurdly solitary promontory, or a farcical star refractory to all constellations. Irresponsible out of melancholy, your life has flouted its moments; now, life is the *piety of duration*, the feeling of a dancing eternity, time transcending itself, and vies with the sun. . . .

Acedia

This stagnation of the organs, this stupor of the faculties, this petrified smile—do they not often remind you of the ennui of the cloisters, hearts abandoned by God, the dryness and idiocy of the monks loathing themselves in the ecstatic transports of masturbation? You are merely a monk without divine hypotheses and without the pride of solitary vice.

Earth, heaven are the walls of your cell, and in the air no breath disturbs, only the absence of orisons prevails. Doomed to the empty hours of eternity, to the periphery of shudders and the mildewed desires that rot at the approach of salvation, you bestir yourself toward a Last Judgment without splendor and trumpets, while your thoughts, for solemnity, have imagined no more than the unreal procession of hopes.

By grace of suffering, souls once flung themselves toward the vaulting arches; you stumble against them now, and you fall back into the world as into a faithless convent, lagging on the boulevard, Order of Lost Creatures—and of your perdition.

Crimes of Courage and Fear

To be afraid is to think of yourself continually, to be unable to imagine an objective course of events. The sensation of the terrible, the sensation that it is all happening *against* you, supposes a world conceived without *indifferent* dangers. The frightened man—victim of an exaggerated subjectivity—believes himself to be, much more than the rest of his kind, the target of hostile events. He encounters the brave man in this error, for the brave man, at the antipodes, sees only invulnerability everywhere. Both have attained the extremity of a self-infatuated consciousness: everything conspires against the one; to the other, everything is favorable. (The brave man is only a braggart who embraces the danger, who flees toward the danger.) One establishes himself negatively at the center of the world, the other positively; but their illusion is the same, their knowledge having an identical point of departure: danger as the only reality. One fears it, the other seeks it out: they cannot conceive a lucid scorn of things, they both relate everything to themselves, they are over-agitated (and all the evil in the world comes from the excess of agitation, from the dynamic fictions of bravery and cowardice). Thus these antinomic and equal examples are the agents of all our troubles, the disturbers of the march of time; they give an affective tinge to the least event and project their fevered intentions upon a universe which—without an abandonment to calm disgusts—is degrading and intolerable. Courage and fear, two poles of the same disease, which consists in granting an abusive sense and seriousness to life. . . . It is the lack of nonchalant bitterness which makes men into sectarian beasts; the subtlest and the crudest crimes are perpetrated by those who take things seriously. Only the dilettante has no taste for blood, he alone is no scoundrel. . . .

Disintoxication

The non-mysterious concerns of human beings may be drawn as clearly as the outlines of this page. . . . What is to be inscribed here but the disgust of generations linked like propositions in the sterile fatality of a syllogism?

The human adventure will certainly come to an end, which we may conceive without being its contemporary. When we have consummated in ourselves the divorce with history, it is quite superfluous to attend the formalities. We need only look at man in the face to detach ourselves from him and to no longer regret his hoaxes. Thousands of years of sufferings, which would have softened the hearts of stones, merely petrified this steely mayfly, monstrous example of evanescence and hardening, driven by one insipid madness, a will to exist at once imperceptible and shameless. When we realize that no human motive is compatible with infinity and that no gesture is worth the trouble of making it, our heart, by its very beating, can no longer conceal its vacuity. Men mingle in a uniform fate as futile, for the indifferent eye, as the stars—or the crosses of a military cemetery. Of all the goals proposed for existence, which one, subjected to analysis, escapes the music-hall or the morgue?

Which fails to reveal us as futile or sinister? And is there a single stroke of magic, is there one charm which can still deceive us?

(When we are forbidden visible prescriptions, we become, like the devil, metaphysically *illegal*; we have left the order of the world: no longer finding a place there, we look at it without recognition; stupefaction turns into a reflex, while our plaintive astonishment, lacking an object, is forever fastened to the Void. We undergo sensations which no longer correspond to things because nothing irritates them any longer; thus we transcend even the dream of the angel of Melancholia, and we regret that Dürer did not languish for eyes even more remote. . . .

When everything seems too concrete, too existent, including our noblest vision, and we sigh for an Indefinite which would proceed from neither life nor death, when every contact with Being is a violation of the soul, the soul has been excluded from the universal jurisdiction and, no longer having any accounting to make or laws to infringe, vies—by melancholy—with the divine omnipotence.)

Itinerary of Hate

I hate no one; but hatred blackens my blood and scorches this skin which the years were powerless to tan. How prevail, under tender or rigorous judgments, over a hideous gloom and the scream of a man flayed alive?

I wanted to love heaven and earth, their exploits and their fevers—and I have found nothing which failed to remind me of death: flowers, stars, faces—symbols of withering, potential slabs of all possible tombs! What is created in life, and ennobles it, tends toward a macabre or mediocre end. The effervescence of hearts has provoked disasters which no demon would have dared conceive. Look upon a mind enflamed and be sure that you will end by being its victim. Those who believe in *their* truth—the only ones whose imprint is retained by the memory of men—leave the earth behind them strewn with corpses. Religions number in their ledgers more murders than the bloodiest tyrannies account for, and those whom humanity has called divine far surpass the most conscientious murderers in their thirst for slaughter.

The man who proposes a new faith is persecuted, until it is his turn to become a persecutor: truths begin by a conflict with the police and end by calling them in; for each absurdity we have suffered for degenerates into a legality, as every martyrdom ends in the paragraphs of the Law, in the insipidities of the calendar, or the nomenclature of the streets. In this world, heaven itself becomes *authority*; and we know ages which lived only by it—Middle Ages more prodigal in wars than the most dissolute epochs, bestial crusades tricked out as sublimities, before which the invasions of the Huns seem the refrains of decadent hordes.

Immaculate exploits decline into public enterprise; consecration dims the most aerial halo. An angel protected by a policeman—that is how truths die, that is how enthusiasms expire. It is enough that a rebellion be right and create adherents, a revelation be propagated and an institution confiscate it, for the once-solitary transports—divided among a few neophyte dreamers—to be corrupted in a prostituted existence. Show me one thing here on earth which has begun well and which has not ended badly. The proudest palpitations are engulfed in a sewer, where they cease throbbing, as though having reached their natural term: this downfall constitutes the heart's drama and the negative meaning of history. Each "ideal" fed, at its beginning, on the blood of its votaries, erodes and collapses when it is adopted by the mob. The font transformed into a spittoon: that is the ineluctable rhythm of "progress". . . .

Under these conditions, upon whom are we to pour out our hatred? No one is responsible for being, and still less for being what he is. Afflicted with existence, each man endures like an animal the consequences which proceed from it. Thus, in a world where everything is detestable, hatred becomes huger than the world and, having transcended its object, cancels itself out.

(It is not our suspect exhaustions or the specific disturbances of our organs which reveal the low point of our vitality; nor is it our perplexities or the variations of the thermometer; but we need merely endure those fits of hatred and pity *without motive*, those non-measurable fevers, to understand that our equilibrium is threatened. To hate everything and to hate yourself, in a frenzy of cannibal rage; to pity everyone and to pity yourself—apparently contradictory impulses, but at their source identical; for we can pity only what we want to do away with, what does not deserve to exist. And in these convulsions, the man who endures them and the universe to which they are addressed are doomed to the same destructive and pitying fury. When, all of a sudden, you are overcome with compassion without knowing for whom, it is because a lassitude of the organs presages a dangerous decline; and when this vague and universal compassion turns toward yourself, you are in the condition of the last and least of men. It is from an enormous physical weakness that this negative solidarity emanates, a solidarity which, in hate or pity, binds us to things. These two frenzies, simultaneous or consecutive, are not so much uncertain symptoms as clear signs of a falling vitality irritated by anything and everything—from undelineated existence to the precision of our own person.

Yet we must not deceive ourselves: these outbreaks are the clearest and the most immoderate, but scarcely the only ones; at different degrees, everything is pathology, except for Indifference.)

"La Perduta Gente"

What a preposterous notion, to draw circles in hell, to make the intensity of the flames vary in its compartments, to hierarchize its torments! The important thing is to be there; the rest—mere *fioriteras* or . . . burns. In the heavenly city—gentler prefiguration of the one below, both being under the same management—the essential thing, too, is not to be something—king, bourgeois, day-laborer—but to adhere to it or to escape it. You can champion some idea or other, have a place or crawl—from the moment your actions and your thoughts serve a form of real or imagined city you are its idolators and its captives. The timidest employee and the wildest anarchist, if they take a different interest here, live as its function: they are both citizens *internally*, though the one prefers his slippers and the other his bomb. The "circles" of the earthly city, like those of the one underground, imprison beings in a damned community, and drag them in the same procession of sufferings, in which to look for nuances would be a waste of time. The man who acquiesces in human affairs—in any form, revolutionary or conservative—consumes himself in a pitiable delectation: he commingles his nobilities and his vulgarities in the confusion of Becoming. . . .

To the dissenter, within or outside the city, reluctant to intervene in the course of great events or small, all modalities of life in common seem equally contemptible. History can offer him only the pale interest of renewed disappointments and anticipated artifices. The man who has lived among men *and still lies in wait for a single unexpected event*—such a man has understood nothing and never will. He is ripe for the City: everything must be given him, every office and every honor. So it is with all men—which explains the longevity of this sublunary hell.

History and Language

Who can resist the autumnal wisdom of the flaccid and *faisandé* civilizations? The Greek's horror, like the belated Roman's, of freshness and the hyperborean reflexes, emanated from a repulsion for dawns, for barbarism overflowing with futures, and for the stupidities of health. The resplendent corruption of every historic late-season is darkened by the proximity of the Scythian. No civilization can draw out an indefinite agony; tribes prowl about, scenting the aromas of perfumed corpses. . . . Thus, the enthusiast of sunsets contemplates the failure of all refinement and the insolent advance of vitality. Nothing left for him to do but collect, from the sum of the future, a few anecdotes. . . . A system of events no longer proves anything: the great deeds have joined the fairy tales and the handbooks. The glorious exploits of the past, like the men who performed them, are still of interest only for the fine words which have consecrated them. Woe to the conqueror without a word to say! Jesus himself, though an indirect dictator for two thousand years, marked the memory of his faithful and of his detractors only by the tatters of paradoxes which strew a biography so adroitly scenic. How inquire about a martyr today if he has not uttered remarks adequate to his sufferings? We keep the memory of past or recent victims only if their language has immortalized the blood which has spattered them. The executioners themselves survive only insofar as they were performers: Nero would be long since forgotten without his outbursts of bloody clowning.

When, at the dying man's bedside, his nearest and dearest bend over his stammerings, it is not so much to decipher in them some last wish, but rather to gather up a good phrase which they can quote later on, in order to honor his memory. If the Roman historians never fail to describe the agony of their emperors, it is in order to place within them a sentence or an exclamation which the latter uttered or were supposed to have uttered. This is true for all deathbeds, even the most ordinary. That life signifies nothing, everyone knows or suspects; let it at least be saved by a turn of phrase! A sentence at the corners of their life—that is about all we ask of the great—and of the small. If they fail this requirement, this obligation, they are lost forever; for we forgive everything, down to crimes, on condition they are exquisitely *glossed*—and glossed over. This is the absolution man grants history as a whole, when no other criterion is seen to be operative and valid, and when he himself, recapitulating the general inanity, finds no other dignity than that of a *littérateur* of failure and an aesthete of bloodshed.

In this world, where sufferings are merged and blurred, only the *Formula* prevails.

Philosophy and Prostitution

The philosopher, disappointed with systems and superstitions but still persevering in the ways of the world, should imitate the sidewalk Pyrrhonism exhibited by the least dogmatic of creatures: the prostitute. Detached from everything and open to everything; espousing her client's mood and ideas; changing tone and face on each occasion; ready to be sad or gay, being indifferent; lavishing sighs out of commercial concern; casting upon the frolic of her superimposed and sincere neighbor an enlightened and artificial gaze—she proposes to the mind a model of behavior which vies with that of the sages. To be without convictions in regard to men and oneself, such is the high lesson of prostitution, peripatetic academy of lucidity, marginal to society—as is philosophy. "Everything I know I learned in the School of Whores!" should be the exclamation of the thinker who accepts everything and rejects everything, when, following their example, he has specialized in the weary smile, when men are to him merely clients, and the world's sidewalks the marketplace where he sells his bitterness, as his companions sell their bodies.

Obsession of the Essential

When every question seems accidental and peripheral, when the mind seeks ever greater problems, it turns out that in its procedure it no longer comes up against any object but the diffuse obstacle of the Void. Thereupon, the philosophic energy, exclusively oriented toward the inaccessible, is exposed to ruin. Scrutinizing things and their temporal pretexts, it imposes salutary embarrassments upon itself; but, if it seeks an increasingly general principle, it is lost and annihilated in the vagueness of the Essential.

Only those who stop apropos in philosophy flourish, those who accept the limitation and the comfort of a reasonable stage of anxiety. Every problem, if we get to the bottom of it, leads to bankruptcy and leaves the intellect exposed: no more questions and no more answers in a space without horizon. The interrogations turn against the mind which has conceived them: it becomes their victim. Everything is hostile to it: its own solitude, its own audacity, the opaque absolute, the unverifiable gods, and the manifest nothingness. Woe to the man who, having arrived at a certain moment of the essential, has not drawn up short! History shows that the thinkers who mounted to the top of the ladder of questions, who set their foot on the last rung, that of the absurd, have bequeathed to posterity only an example of sterility, whereas their confreres, stopping halfway up, have fertilized the mind's growth; they have *served* their kind, they have transmitted some well-turned idol, some polished superstitions, some errors disguised as principles, and a system of hopes. Had they embraced the dangers of an excessive progression, this scorn of charitable mistakes would have rendered them disastrous to others and to themselves; they would have inscribed their names on the confines of the universe and of thought—unhealthy seekers and arid reprobates, amateurs of fruitless dizziness, hunters of dreams it is not permitted to dream. . . .

Ideas refractory to the Essential are the only ones to have a purchase on men. What would they do with a region of thought where even the man who aspires to settle by natural inclination or morbid thirst is jeopardized? No breathing in a realm alien to the usual doubts. And if certain minds locate themselves outside the agreed upon inquiries, it is because an instinct rooted in the depths of matter, or a vice rising out of a cosmic disease, has taken possession of them and has led them to an order of reflections so exigent and so enormous that death itself seems of no importance, the elements of destiny mere nonsense, and the apparatus of metaphysics no more than utilitarian and suspect. This obsession with a last frontier, this progress in the void involve the most dangerous form of sterility, beside which nothingness itself seems a promise of fecundity. The man who is *difficult* in what he does—in his task or his adventure— has merely to transplant his demand for *finish* to the universal level in order to be no longer able to complete either his work or his life.

Metaphysical anguish derives from the condition of a supremely scrupulous artisan whose object would be nothing less than *being*. By dint of analysis, he achieves the impossibility of composing, of perfecting a miniature of the universe. The artist abandoning his poem, exasperated by the indigence of words, prefigures the confusion of the mind discontented within the context of the existent. Incapacity to organize the elements—as stripped of meaning and savor as the words which express them—leads to the revelation of the void. Thus the rhymer withdraws into silence or into impenetrable artifices. In the face of the universe, the over-exigent mind suffers a defeat like Mallarmé's in the face of art. It is panic before an object which is no longer an object, which can no longer be manipulated, for—ideally—its limits have been transcended. Those who do not remain *inside* the reality they cultivate, those who transcend the task of existing, must either compromise with the inessential, reverse gears and take their places in the eternal farce, or accept all the consequences of a severed condition which is either superfetation or tragedy, depending on whether it is contemplated or endured.

Felicity of Epigones

Is there a pleasure more subtly ambiguous than to watch the ruin of a myth? What dilapidation of hearts in order to beget it, what excesses of intolerance in order to make it respected, what terror for those who do not assent to it, and what expense of hopes for those who watch it . . . expire! Intelligence flourishes only in the ages when beliefs wither, when their articles and their precepts slacken, when their rules collapse. Every period's ending is the mind's paradise, for the mind regains its play and its whims only within an organism in utter dissolution. The man who has the misfortune to belong to a period of creation and fecundity suffers its limitations and its ruts; slave of a unilateral vision, he is enclosed within a limited horizon. The most fertile moments in history were at the same time the most airless; they prevailed like a fatality, a blessing for the naive mind, mortal to an amateur of intellectual space. Freedom has scope only among the disabused and sterile epigones, among the intellects of belated epochs, epochs whose style is coming apart and is no longer inspired except by a certain ironic indulgence.

To belong to a church uncertain of its god—after once imposing that god by fire and sword—should be the ideal of every detached mind. When a myth languishes and turns diaphanous, and the institution which sustains it turns clement and tolerant, problems acquire a pleasant elasticity. The weak point of a faith, the diminished degree of its vigor set up a tender void in men's souls and render them receptive, though without permitting them to be blind, yet, to the superstitions which lie in wait for the future they darken already. The mind is soothed only by those agonies of history which precede the insanity of every dawn. . . .

Ultimate Audacity

If it is true that Nero exclaimed, "Lucky Priam, who saw the ruin of your country!" let us grant him the merit of having acceded to a sublime defiance, to the last hypostasis of the *beau geste* and lugubrious grandiloquence. After such a phrase, so marvelously appropriate in an emperor's mouth, one is entitled to banality; one is even compelled to it. Who could pretend to further extravagance? The petty accidents of our triviality force us to admire this cruel and histrionic Caesar (all the more in that his madness has known a glory greater than the sighs of his victims, written history being at least as inhuman as the events which provoke it). Beside his, all *attitudes* seem antics. And if it is true that he set Rome on fire in imitation of the *Iliad*, was there ever a more *tangible* homage to a work of art? In any case, it is the one example of literary criticism *at work*, of an *active* aesthetic judgment.

The effect a book has upon us is real only if we crave to imitate its plot, to kill if its hero kills, to be jealous if he is jealous, to take sick and die if he suffers and expires. But all this, for us, remains in the potential state or declines to *dead letters*; only Nero grants himself literature as a spectacle; his *accounting* is made with the ashes of his contemporaries and of his capital. . . .

Such words and such actions had to be uttered and performed at least once. A criminal took them upon himself. This can console us, indeed it must, or else how should we resume our customary behavior and our convenient and prudent truths?

Effigy of the Failure

Having a horror of any action, he keeps telling himself: "Movement, what folly!" It is not so much events which vex him as the notion of participating in them; and he bestirs himself only in order to turn away from them. His sneers have devastated life before he has exhausted its juice. He is a crossroads Ecclesiast who finds in the universal meaninglessness an excuse for his defeats. Eager to find everything unimportant, he succeeds easily, the evidence preponderant on his side. In the battle of arguments, he is always the winner, as he is always the loser in action: he is "right," he rejects everything—and everything rejects him. He has prematurely compromised what must not be compromised in order to live—and since his talent was over-enlightened as to his own functions, he has squandered it lest it dribble away into the inanity of a work. Bearing the image of what he might have been as a stigma and a halo, he blushes and flatters himself on the excellence of his sterility, forever alien to naive seductions, the one free man among the helots of Time. He extracts his liberty from the enormity of his lack of accomplishments; he is an infinite and pitiable god whom no creation limits, no creature worships, and whom no one spares. The scorn he has poured out on others is returned by them. He expiates only the actions he has not performed, though their number exceeds the calculations of his wounded pride. But at the end, as a kind of consolation, and at the close of a life without honors, he wears his uselessness like a crown.

("What's the use?"—the Failure's adage, the maxim of death's timeserver. . . . What a stimulant when you begin to suffer its obsession! For death, before weighing too heavily upon us, enriches us, our powers grow at its contact; then, it performs its work of destruction upon us. The evidence of the uselessness of all effort, and that sensation of a future corpse already rising into the present and filling time's horizon, end by benumbing our ideas, our hopes, and our muscles, so that the excess of energy provoked by the quite recent obsession is converted—when that obsession is irrevocably implanted in the mind—into a stagnation of our vitality. Thus this obsession incites us to become everything and nothing. Normally it should confront us with the one choice possible: the convent or the cabaret. But when we can evade it by neither eternity nor pleasures, when, attacked in the midst of life, we are as far from heaven as from vulgarity, it transforms us into that kind of decomposed hero who promises everything and accomplishes nothing: idle men wasting their breath in the Void; vertical carrion whose sole activity is reduced to thinking that they will cease to be. . . .)

Conditions of Tragedy

If Jesus had ended his career upon the Cross, if he had not been committed to resuscitation—what a splendid tragic hero! His divine aspect has cost literature an admirable subject. Thereby he shares the fate, aesthetically mediocre, of all *just men*. Like everything which perpetuates itself in men's hearts, like everything which is exposed to worship and does not irremediably die, he does not lend himself to that vision of a total end which marks out a tragic destiny. For that it would have been necessary that Jesus have no followers and that the transfiguration did not come to raise him to an illicit halo. Nothing more alien to tragedy than the notion of redemption, of salvation and immortality! The hero succumbs under the weight of his own actions, without its being granted him to evade his death by some supernatural grace; he continues—as an *existence*—in no way whatever, he remains *distinct* in men's memory as a *spectacle* of suffering; having no disciples, his sterile destiny proves fruitful to nothing but other people's imagination. Macbeth collapses without the hope of a redemption: there is no *extreme unction* in tragedy. . . .

The nature of a faith, even if it must fail, is to elude the Irreparable. (What could Shakespeare have done with a martyr?) The true hero fights and dies in the name of his destiny, and not in the name of a belief. His existence eliminates any notion of an escape; the paths which do not lead him to death are dead ends to him; he works at his "biography"; he tends to his denouement and instinctively manages everything to bring about events fatal to himself. Fatality being his vital juice, every way out can be no more than a disloyalty to his destruction. Thus the man of destiny is never converted to any belief whatever: he would thereby spoil his end. And, if he were immobilized on the cross, it is not he who would raise his eyes to heaven: his own history is his sole absolute, as his *will* to tragedy is his sole desire. . . .

The Immanent Lie

To live signifies to believe and to hope—to lie and to lie *to oneself*. This is why the most truthful image ever created of man remains that of the Knight of the Doleful Countenance, that Don whom we find in even the most fulfilled of the sages. The painful episode around the Cross and the other more majestic one crowned by Nirvana participate in the same unreality, though they have been granted a symbolic quality denied by the sequel of the poor hidalgo's adventures. Not all men can succeed: the fecundity of their lies varies. . . . One deception triumphs: there results a religion, a doctrine, or a myth—and a host of adepts; another fails: then it is only a divagation, a theory, or a fiction. Only inert things *add* nothing to what they are: a stone does not lie; it interests no one—whereas life indefatigably invents: life is the *novel* of matter.

A dust infatuated with ghosts—such is man: his absolute image, ideally lifelike, would be incarnated in a Don Quixote seen by Aeschylus. . . .

(If life occupies the first place in the hierarchy of lies, love comes immediately afterward, lie within the lie. Expression of our hybrid position, love is surrounded by an apparatus of beatitudes and torments thanks to which we find in someone a substitute for ourselves. By what hoax do two eyes turn us away from our solitude? Is there any failure more humiliating for the mind? Love lulls knowledge; wakened, knowledge kills love. Unreality cannot triumph indefinitely, even disguised in the appearances of the most exalting lie. And moreover who would have an illusion solid enough to find in the *other* what he has vainly sought in himself? Would a furnace of guts afford what the whole universe could not give us? And yet this is the actual basis of this common, and supernatural, anomaly: to solve *à deux*—or rather, to suspend—all enigmas; by means of an imposture, to forget that fiction in which life is steeped; by a double murmur to fill the general vacuity; and—parody of ecstasy—to drown oneself at last in the sweat of some accomplice or other. . . .)

The Coming of Consciousness

How much our instincts must have had to be blunted and their functioning slackened before consciousness extended its control over the sum of our actions and our thoughts! The first natural reaction *suppressed* involved all the postponements of vital activity, all our failures in the immediate. Man—an animal with retarded desires—is a lucid nothingness encircling everything and encircled by nothing, who surveys all objects and possesses none.

Compared to the coming of consciousness, other events are of a minor importance or none at all. But this advent, in contradiction with the data of life, constitutes a dangerous explosion at the heart of the animate world, a scandal in biology. Nothing suggested its imminence: natural automatism suggested no likelihood of an animal flinging itself beyond matter. The gorilla losing its fur and replacing it by ideals, the gorilla in gloves, forging gods, aggravating his grimaces, and adoring the heavens—how much nature was to suffer, and will suffer still, before such a fall! This is because consciousness leads far and permits everything. For the animal, life is an absolute; for man, it is an absolute and a pretext. In the evolution of the universe, there is no phenomenon more important than this possibility, reserved for us, of converting every object into a pretext, to *play* with our everyday undertakings and our last ends, to put on the same level, by the divinity of whim, a god and a broomstick.

And man will be rid of his ancestors—and of nature—only when he has liquidated in himself every vestige of the Unconditioned, when his life and that of others will seem no more to him than a set of strings he will pull for laughs, in an amusement for the end of time. Then he will be the *pure being*. Consciousness will have played its role. . . .

The Arrogance of Prayer

When we reach the limits of monologue, the confines of solitude, we invent—for lack of another interlocutor—God, supreme pretext of dialogue. So long as you name Him, your madness is well disguised, and . . . all is permitted. The true believer is scarcely to be distinguished from the madman; but his madness is legal, acknowledged; he would end up in an asylum if his aberrations were pure of all faith. But God covers them, legitimizes them. The pride of a conqueror pales beside the ostentation of a believer who addresses himself to the Creator. How can one dare so much? And how could modesty be a virtue of temples, when a decrepit old woman who imagines Infinity within reach raises herself by prayer to a level of audacity to which no tyrant has ever laid claim?

I should sacrifice the world's empire for one single moment when my clasped hands would implore the great Responsible for our riddles and our banalities. Yet this moment constitutes the common quality—and in a sense the *official* time—of any believer. But the man who is truly modest keeps repeating to himself: "Too humble to pray, too inert to step across the church threshold, I resign myself to my shadow, and seek no capitulation from God before my prayers." And to those who offer him immortality he replies: "My pride is not inexhaustible: its resources are limited. You imagine, in the name of faith, that you are conquering your *self*; in fact, you seek to perpetuate it in eternity, this earthly duration being insufficient for you. Your vainglory exceeds in refinement all the ambitions of the age. What dream of fame, compared to yours, fails to turn out deception and smoke? Your faith is merely a *folie de grandeurs* tolerated by the community, because it has taken disguised paths; but your dust is your one obsession: greedy for the timeless, you persecute the time which disperses it. The Beyond alone is spacious enough for your cravings; the earth and its moments seem too fragile for you. The megalomania of monasteries exceeds all that the sumptuous fevers of palaces ever imagined. The man who does not assent to his nothingness is mentally diseased. And the believer, of all men, is the least disposed to assent to it. The will to endure, pushed to such lengths, terrifies me. I reject the morbid seduction of an indefinite Me . . . I want to wallow in my mortality. I want to remain *normal*."

(Lord, give me the capacity of never praying, spare me the insanity of all worship, let this temptation of love pass from me which would deliver me forever unto You. Let the void spread between my heart and heaven! I have no desire to people my deserts by Your presence, to tyrannize my nights by Your light, to dissolve my Siberias beneath Your sun. Lonelier than You, I want my hands pure, the contrary of Yours which were forever corrupted by kneading the earth and busying themselves with the world's affairs. I ask Your stupid omnipotence for nothing but the respect of my solitude and my torments. What have I to do with Your words? And I fear the madness which would make me hear them. Grant me the miracle gathered before the first moment, the peace which You could not tolerate and which incited You to breach the nothingness in order to make way for this carnival of time, and thereby to condemn me to the universe—to humiliation and the shame of Being.)

Lypemania

Why do you lack the strength to escape the obligation to breathe? Why still endure that solidified air which clogs your lungs and crushes your flesh? How vanquish these opaque hopes and these petrified ideas, when turn and turn about you imitate the solitude of a crag or the isolation of a wad of spittle frozen on the edge of the world? You are farther from yourself than an undiscovered planet, and your organs, turned toward the graveyards, envy their dynamism. . . .

Open your veins in order to flood this page which infuriates you the way the seasons do? Absurd effort! Your blood, faded by white nights, has suspended its flow. . . . Nothing will waken in you the need for living and dying, extinguished by the years, forever slaked by those springs without murmur or prestige at which men quench their thirst. Monster with mute, dry lips, you will remain beyond the sounds of life and death, beyond even the sound of tears. . . .

(The true greatness of the saints consists in that incomparable power of defeating the Fear of Ridicule. We cannot weep without shame; they invoked the "gift of tears." A preoccupation with honor in our "dryness" immobilizes us into the spectators of our bitter and repressed infinity, our streams that do not flow. Yet the eyes' function is not to see but to weep; and really to *see* we must close them: that is the condition of ecstasy, of the one revealing vision, whereas perception is exhausted in the horror of the *déjà vu*, of an irreparable recognition scene which occurred at the beginning. . . .

For the man who has foreseen the world's futile disasters, and to whom knowledge has afforded only the confirmation of an innate disenchantment, the scruples which keep him from weeping accentuate his predestination to melancholy. And if he actually envies the saints' exploits, it is not so much for their disgust with appearances or their transcendent appetite, but rather for their victory over that fear of ridicule, which he cannot avoid and which keeps him on this side of the supernatural indecorum of tears.)

Everyday Curse

To repeat to yourself a thousand times a day: "Nothing on earth has any worth," to keep finding yourself at the same point, to circle stupidly as a top, eternally. . . . For there is no progression in the notion of universal vanity, nor conclusion; and as far as we venture in such ruminations, our knowledge makes no gain: it is in its present state as rich and as void as at its point of departure. It is a surcease within the incurable, a leprosy of the mind, a revelation by stupor. A simple-minded person, an idiot who has experienced an illumination and grown used to it with no means of leaving it behind, of recovering his vague and comfortable condition—such is the state of the man who finds himself committed in spite of himself to the perception of universal futility. Abandoned by his nights, virtually a victim of a lucidity which smothers him, what is he to do with this day which never manages to end? When will the light stop shedding its beams, deadly to the memory of a night world anterior to all that was? How far away chaos is, restful and calm, the chaos dating from before the terrible Creation, or sweeter still, the chaos of mental nothingness!

Defense of Corruption

If we put in one pan the evil the "pure" have poured out upon the world, and in the other the evil that has come from men without principles and without scruples, the scale would tip toward the first.

In the mind that proposes it, every recipe for salvation erects a guillotine. . . . The disasters of corrupt periods have less gravity than the scourges caused by the ardent ones; mud is more agreeable than blood; and there is more mildness in vice than in virtue, more humanity in depravity than in austerity. The man who rules and believes in nothing—behold the model of a paradise of forfeiture, a sovereign solution to history. Opportunists have saved nations; heroes have ruined them. To feel that one is a contemporary not of the Revolution and of Bonaparte, but of Fouché and of Talleyrand: the only thing lacking in the latters' versatility was a drop of melancholy for them to suggest by their actions a whole Art of Living.

It is the dissolute ages which can claim the merit of laying bare the essence of life, of showing us that everything is only *farce* or *gall*—and that no event is worth being touched up: it is necessarily execrable. The embellished lie of the great periods, of this century, that king, that pope. . . . The "truth" appears only at those moments when men's minds, forgetting the constructive delirium, let themselves slip back into the dissolution of morals, of ideals, and of beliefs. To know is to *see*; it is neither to hope nor to try.

The stupidity which characterizes history's peaks has no equivalent but the ineptitude of those who are its agents. It is out of a lack of finesse that we carry our actions and our thoughts to their conclusions. A detached mind shrinks from tragedy and apotheosis: disgraces and palms exasperate such a spirit as much as banality. *To go too far* is to give an infallible proof of bad taste. The aesthete has a horror of blood, sublimity, and heroes. . . . He still values only the dissipated. . . .

The Obsolete Universe

The aging process in the verbal universe follows a much more accelerated rhythm than in the material one. Words, too often repeated, weaken and die, whereas monotony constitutes the very law of matter. The mind should have an infinite dictionary, but its means are limited to a few expressions trivialized by usage. Hence the *new*, requiring strange combinations, forces words into unexpected functions: *originality is reduced to the torment of the adjective and to the suggestive impropriety of metaphor.* Put words in their place: that is the everyday graveyard of Speech. What is *consecrated* in a language constitutes its death: an *anticipated* word is a defunct one; only its artificial use imbues it with a new vigor, until it is commonly adopted, worn, corrupted. . . . The mind is *precious*—or it is not the mind, whereas nature lolls in the simplicity of its always identical means.

What we call *our* life, in relation to "life," is an incessant creation of vogues with the help of an artificially manipulated speech; it is a proliferation of futilities, without which we should have to expire in a yawn that would engulf history and matter alike. If man invents a new physics, it is not so much to arrive at a valid explanation of nature as to escape the boredom of the understood, habitual, vulgarly irreducible universe, to which he arbitrarily attributes as many dimensions as we project adjectives upon an inert thing we are tired of seeing and suffering as it was seen and suffered by the stupidity of our ancestors or of our immediate predecessors. Woe to the man who, having understood this masquerade, withdraws from it! He will have encroached upon the secret of his vitality—and he will join the motionless, unaffected truth of those in whom the wellsprings of the Precious have dried up, and whose mind is etiolated for want of the artificial.

(It is only too legitimate to imagine the moment when life will no longer be the fashion, when it will fall into desuetude like the moon or tuberculosis after the abuses of romanticism: life will then crown the anachronism of the denuded symbols and the unmasked diseases; it will once again become *itself*: an ill without prestige, a fatality without luster. And that moment is only too foreseeable when no hope will reappear in men's hearts, when the earth will be as glacial as its creatures, when no dream will come back to embellish the sterile immensity of it all. Humanity will blush to beget when it sees things as they are. Life without the sap of mistakes and deceptions, life ceasing to be a vogue, will find no clemency at the mind's tribunal. But finally, that mind itself will give way: it is only an excuse in the void, as life is only a prejudice.

History sustains itself as long as above our transitory fashions, of which events are the shadow, a more general fashion floats like a constant; but when this constant is generally exposed as a simple whim, when the knowledge of the mistake of living becomes common property and unanimous truth, where shall we seek resources in order to engender or even to sketch out an action, the simulacrum of a gesture? By what art survive our lucid instincts and our perspicacious hearts? By what miracle reanimate a future temptation in an obsolete universe?)

Decrepit Man

I no longer want to collaborate with the light or use the jargon of life. And I shall no longer say "I am" without blushing. The immodesty of the breath, the scandal of the lungs are linked to the abuse of an auxiliary verb. . . .

The time is past when man thought of himself in terms of a dawn; behold him resting on an anemic matter, open to his true duty, the duty of studying his loss, and of rushing into it . . . behold him on the threshold of a new epoch: the epoch of *Self-Pity*. And this Pity is his second fall, more distinct and more humiliating than the first: it is a fall without redemption. Vainly he inspects the horizons: a thousand saviors are silhouetted there, humbug saviors, themselves unconsoled. He turns away in order to prepare himself, in his overripe soul, for the sweetness of corruption. . . . Having reached the intimacy of his autumn, he wavers between Appearance and Nothingness, between the deceptive form of Being and its absence: vibration between two unrealities. . . .

Consciousness occupies the void which follows the mind's erosion of existence. It takes the obnubilation of an idiot or a believer to participate in "reality," which collapses at the approach of the slightest doubt, a suspicion of improbability, or a shudder of anguish—so many rudiments which prefigure consciousness and which, once *developed*, beget it, define and exasperate it. Under the effect of this consciousness, of this incurable presence, man gains access to his highest privilege: that of destroying himself. Nature's privileged patient, man corrupts her sap; abstract vice of the instincts, he destroys their vigor. The universe withers at his touch and time decamps. . . . He could fulfill himself—and descend the further slope—only on the wreck of the elements. His work completed, he is ripe for disappearance; through how many centuries more will his death rattle sound?

2

THE SECOND-HAND THINKER

Ideas are substitutes for griefs.
—Marcel Proust

The Second-Hand Thinker

I live in expectation of the Idea; I foresee it, close in upon it, get a grip—and cannot formulate it, it escapes me, does not yet belong to me: might I have conceived it in my absence? And how, once imminent and vague, to make it present and luminous in the intelligible agony of expression? What conditions should I hope for if it is to bloom—and decay?

Anti-philosopher, I abhor every *indifferent* idea: I am not always despondent, hence I do not always think. When I *consider* ideas, they seem even more useless than things; hence I have loved only the elucubrations of the great invalids, the ruminations of insomnia, the flashes of an incurable fear, and the doubts intersected by sighs. The amount of chiaroscuro an idea harbors is the only index of its profundity, as the despairing accent of its playfulness is the index of its fascination. How many white nights does your nocturnal past conceal? That is how we ought to confront every thinker. The man who thinks *when he wants to* has nothing to tell us: above—or rather, *alongside*—his thoughts, he is not *responsible* for them, not committed to them, neither wins nor loses by risking himself in a struggle in which he himself is not his own enemy. It costs him nothing to believe in Truth. Which is not the case for a mind where *true* and *false* have ceased to be superstitions; destroyer of all criteria, such a mind *verifies itself*, like invalids and poets; it thinks by accident: the glory of a discomfort or of a delirium suffices. Is not an indigestion richer in ideas than a parade of concepts? Malfunctions of our organs determine the fruitfulness of our minds: the man who does not *feel* his body will never be in a position to conceive a living thought; he will wait to no purpose for the advantageous surprise of some disadvantage. . . .

95

In affective indifference, ideas assume a profile; yet none can take shape: it is up to melancholy to afford a climate to their blossoming. They require a certain tonality, a certain color in order to vibrate, to shine. To be sterile a long time is to lie in wait for them, to yearn for them without being able to compromise them in a formula. The mind's "seasons" are conditioned by an organic rhythm; it is not up to "me" to be naive or cynical: *my truths are the sophisms of my enthusiasm or of my dejection.* I exist, I feel, and I think according to the moment—and in spite of myself. Time constitutes me; in vain I oppose myself—and *I am.* My undesired present unfolds, unfolds *me*; unable to command it, I comment upon it; slave of my thoughts, I play with them, fatality's buffoon. . . .

Advantages of Debility

The individual who fails to transcend his quality as a splendid example, a finished model, and whose existence is identified with his vital destiny, locates himself outside the mind. Ideal masculinity—obstacle to the perception of nuance—involves an insensitivity to the aspect of the *everyday supernatural,* from which art draws its substance. The more one is a *nature,* the less one is an artist. Homogeneous, undifferentiated, opaque vigor was idolized by the world of legends, by the fantasies of mythology. When the Greeks turned to speculation, the cult of the anemic ephebe replaced that of the giants; and the heroes themselves, sublime dolts in Homer's time, became, thanks to tragedy, bearers of torments and doubts incompatible with their rough nature.

Internal wealth results from conflicts sustained within oneself; now, the vitality which is entirely self-possessed knows only external struggle, the attack upon the object. In the male weakened by a dose of femininity, two tendencies are at grips: by what is passive in himself he apprehends a whole world of relinquishment; by what is imperious, he converts his will into law. As long as his instincts remain unslaked, he concerns only the species; once a secret dissatisfaction creeps in, he becomes a *conqueror.* The mind justifies, explains, and excuses him, and classifying him among the superior simpletons, abandons him to History's curiosity—the investigation of stupidity in action. . . .

The man whose existence does not constitute a disease both vigorous and vague can never establish himself among problems nor know their dangers. The condition favorable to the search for truth or for expression is to be found halfway between man and woman: the gaps in "virility" are the seat of the mind. . . . If the pure female, whom we can accuse of no sexual or psychic anomaly, is internally emptier than an animal, the intact male fits the definition of "cretin." Consider any human being who has caught your attention or roused your fervor: something in his mechanism has been unhinged *to his advantage*. We rightly scorn those who have not made use of their defects, who have not exploited their deficiencies, and have not been enriched by their losses, as we despise any man who does not suffer at being a man or simply at being. Hence no graver insult can be inflicted than to call someone "happy," no greater flattery than to grant him a "vein of melancholy". . . . This is because gaiety is linked to no important action and because, except for the mad, no one laughs when he is alone.

"Inner life" is the prerogative of the delicate, those tremulous wretches subject to an epilepsy with neither froth nor falling: the biologically sound being scorns "depth," is incapable of it, sees in it a suspect dimension which jeopardizes the spontaneity of his actions. Nor is he mistaken: with the retreat into the self begins the individual's drama—his glory and his decline; isolated from the anonymous flux, from the utilitarian trickle of life, he frees himself from *objective goals*. A civilization is "affected" when its delicate members set the tone for it; but thanks to them, it has definitively triumphed over nature—and collapses. An extreme example of refinement unites in himself the *exalté* and the sophist: he no longer adheres to his impulses, cultivates without crediting them; this is the omniscient debility of twilight ages, prefiguration of man's eclipse. The delicate allow us to glimpse the moment when janitors will be tormented by aesthetes' scruples; when farmers, bent double by doubts, will no longer have the vigor to guide the plow; when every human being, gnawed by lucidity and drained of instincts, will be wiped out without the strength to regret the flourishing darkness of their illusions. . . .

The Parasite of Poets

I. There can be no issue in a poet's life. It is from everything he has not undertaken, from all the moments fed on the inaccessible, that his power comes to him. If he finds existence a disadvantage, his expressive faculties are thereby reinforced, his inspiration dilated.

A biography is legitimate only if it focuses the elasticity of a fate, the sum of variables it contains. But the poet follows a line of fatality whose rigor nothing inflects. Life belongs to dolts; and it is in order to fill out the life they have not had that we have invented *the lives of the poets*. . . .

Poetry expresses the essence of what cannot be possessed; its ultimate meaning: the impossibility of all "actuality." Joy is not a poetic sentiment (though it proceeds from a sector of the lyric universe in which chance unites, in one and the same bundle, flames and fatuities). Who has ever read a song of hope which failed to inspire a sensation of discomfort, even of disgust? And how sing a presence, when the *possible* itself is shadowed with vulgarity? Between poetry and hope, complete incompatibility: hence the poet is a prey to an ardent decomposition. Who would dare to wonder how he has experienced life when it is by death that he has been alive at all? When he succumbs to the temptation of happiness—he belongs to comedy. . . . But if, on the other hand, flames spring up from his wounds and he sings felicity—that voluptuous incandescence of woe—he rescues himself from the nuance of vulgarity inherent in any positive accent. Thus a Hölderlin withdrawing to a dream Greece and transfiguring love by purer intoxications, by those of unreality. . . .

The poet would be an odious deserter of reality if in his flight he failed to take his suffering alone. Unlike the mystic or the sage, he cannot escape himself, nor leave the stage of his own obsession: even his ecstasies are incurable, and harbingers of disasters. Unable to run away, for him everything is possible, except life. . . .

II. This is how I recognize an authentic poet: by frequenting him, living a long time in the intimacy of his work, *something* changes in myself: not so much my inclinations or my tastes as my very blood, as if a subtle disease had been injected to alter its course, its density and nature. Valéry and Stefan George leave us where we picked them up, or else make us more demanding on the formal level of the mind: they are geniuses we have no *need* of, they are merely artists. But a Shelley, but a Baudelaire, but a Rilke intervene in the deepest part of our organism which annexes them as it would a vice. In their vicinity, a body is fortified, then weakens and disintegrates. For the poet is an agent of destruction, a virus, a disguised disease, and the gravest danger, though a wonderfully vague one, for our red corpuscles. To live around him is to feel your blood run thin, to dream a paradise of anemia, and to hear, in your veins, the rustle of tears. . . .

III. Whereas verse permits everything—you can pour into it tears, shames, ecstasies, complaints above all—prose forbids you to give vent, to lament: its conventional abstraction is opposed to *overflowing*. Prose requires other truths: verifiable, deduced, measured. But what if you were to steal those of poetry, if you pillaged its substance and dared as much as the poets? Why not insinuate into discourse their indecencies, their humiliations, their grimaces, and their sighs? Why not be decomposed, rotten, corpse, angel, or Satan in the language of the vulgar, and pathetically betray so many aerial and sinister moods? Much more than in the school of the philosophers, it is in the academy of poets that we learn the courage of intelligence and the audacity to be ourselves. Their "affirmations" outdo the most strangely impertinent sayings of the ancient sophists. No one adopts them: has there ever been a single thinker who went as far as Baudelaire or who steeled himself to systematize a Lear's howl, Hamlet's soliloquy? Nietzsche perhaps before his end, but unfortunately he kept harping on his prophet's string. . . . And if we looked among the saints? Certain frenzies of Teresa of Avila or Angela of Foligno. . . . But here we meet God too frequently—God, that *consoling blank* who, reinforcing their courage, diminishes its quality. To advance without convictions and alone among the truths is not given to a man, nor even to a saint; sometimes, though, to a poet. . . .

I can imagine a thinker exclaiming in an impulse of pride: "I'd like a poet to make his fate out of my thoughts!" But for such an aspiration to be legitimate, he himself would have to have frequented the poets a long time, he would have to have borrowed from them the joys of malediction, and given back, abstract and completed, the image of their own defections or their own deliriums; above all he would have to have succumbed on the threshold of song and, a living anthem *this side* of inspiration, to have known *the regret of not being a poet*, of not being initiated into the "science of tears," the scourges of the heart, the formal orgies, the immortalities of the moment. . . .

Many times I have dreamed of a melancholy and erudite monster, versed in all idioms, familiar with numbers and souls alike, who would wander the world feeding on poisons, fervors, ecstasies, crossing Persias, Chinas, defunct Indies, and dying Europes—many times I have dreamed of a friend of the poets who would have known them all out of his despair at not being one of them.

Tribulations of an Alien

Offspring of some wretched tribe, he prowls the boulevards of the West. Cherishing one country after the next, he no longer hopes for any; stuck in a timeless twilight citizen of the world—and of no world—he is ineffectual, nameless, powerless. . . . Peoples without a destiny cannot give one to their sons who, thirsting for other horizons, attach themselves to a fate and ultimately exhaust it to finish their days as ghosts of their admirations and their exhaustions. Having nothing to love *at home,* they locate their love elsewhere, in other lands, where their fervor astonishes the natives. Overworked, the feelings erode and disintegrate, admiration first of all. . . . And the Alien who dispersed himself on so many highways of the world, exclaims: "I have set up countless idols for myself, have raised too many altars everywhere, and I have knelt before a host of gods. Now, weary of worship, I have squandered my share of delirium. One has resources only for the absolutes of one's breed; a soul—like a country—flourishes only within its frontiers. I am paying for having crossed them, for having made the Indefinite into a fatherland, and foreign divinities into a cult, for having prostrated myself before ages which excluded my ancestors. Where I come from I can no longer say: in the temples I am without belief; in the cities, without ardor; among my kind, without curiosity; on the earth, without certitudes. Give me a *specific* desire and I could shake the world to its foundations. Release me from this shame of actions which makes me perform, every morning, the farce of resurrection and, every night, that of entombment; in the interval, nothing but this torment in the shroud of ennui. . . . I dream of wanting—and all I want seems to me worthless. Like a vandal corroded by melancholy, I proceed without a goal, self without a self, toward some unknown corner . . . in order to discover an abandoned god, a god who is his own atheist, and to fall asleep in the shadow of his last doubts and his last miracles."

Ennui of Conquerors

Paris weighed on Napoleon, by his own admission, like a "leaden garment": for which ten million men were to die. This is the balance sheet of the *mal du siècle* when a René on horseback becomes its agent. Born of the idleness of the eighteenth-century salons, this disease, in the indolence of an over-lucid aristocracy, extended its ravages deep into the countryside: peasants were to pay with their blood for a mode of sensibility alien to their nature and, with them, a whole continent. The exceptional natures in which Ennui insinuated itself, horrified by any one place and obsessed by a perpetual elsewhere, exploited the enthusiasm of the nations only to multiply their graveyards. This *condottière* who wept over Werther and Ossian, this Obermann who projected his void into space and who, according to Josephine, was capable of no more than a few moments of *abandon,* had as his unavowed mission to depopulate the earth. The dreaming conqueror is the greatest calamity for men; they are no less eager to idolize him, fascinated as they are by distorted projects, ruinous ideals, unhealthy ambitions. No *reasonable* being was ever the object of worship, left a name, or marked a single event with his individual stamp. Imperturbable before a precise conception or a transparent idol, the mob is roused by the unverifiable, by false mysteries. Who ever died in the name of *rigor?* Each generation raises monuments to the executioners of the one which preceded it. It is nonetheless true that the victims were willing enough to be immolated once they believed in glory, in that victory of one man alone, that defeat of all. . . .

   Humanity adores only those who cause it to perish. Reigns in which citizens died in their sleep do not figure in history, nor the wise prince, inveterately scorned by his subjects; the crowd loves the fictive, even at its expense, the scandal of behavior constituting the web of human curiosity and the underground current of every event. The unfaithful woman and the cuckold provide comedy and tragedy, even the epic, the quasi-totality of their motifs. Since virtue has neither biography nor charm, from the *Iliad* to vaudeville, only the luster of dishonor has entertained and intrigued. Hence it is quite natural that humanity should have offered itself up to the conquerors, that it should seek to be trampled underfoot, that a nation without tyrants should never be talked about, that the sum of iniquities a people commits should be the sole index of its presence and of its vitality. A nation which no longer rapes is in its decadence; the number of rapes reveals its instincts, and its future. Find out in which war it has stopped practicing, on a large scale, this variety of crime: you will have found the first symbol of its decline; find out at what moment love has become for a nation a ceremonial, and the bed a condition of orgasm, and you will identify the beginning of its deficiencies and the end of its barbaric inheritance.

   Universal history: history of Evil. Take away the disasters from human evolution and you might as well conceive of nature without seasons. If you have not contributed to a catastrophe, you will vanish without a trace. We interest others by the misfortune we spread around us. "I never made anyone suffer!"—an exclamation forever alien to a creature of flesh and blood. When we feel enthusiasm for a character of the past, or the present, we *unconsciously* ask ourselves: "For how many people was he the cause of disaster?" Who knows if each of us doesn't aspire to the privilege of killing all his kind? But this privilege is assigned to very few, and never integrally: this restriction alone explains why the earth is still inhabited. Indirect murderers, we constitute an inert mass, a multitude of objects confronting Time's true subjects, the great criminals who came to something.

But we can take comfort: our descendants, remote or immediate, will avenge us. For it is not difficult to imagine the moment when men will cut each other's throats out of disgust with themselves, when Ennui will get the best of their prejudices and their diffidences, when they will run out into the street to slake their thirst for blood, and when the destructive dream prolonged for so many generations will become the universal reality. . . .

Music and Skepticism

I have searched for Doubt in all the arts, have found it there only disguised, furtive, breaking out during the entr'actes of inspiration, rising from slackened impulse; but I have given up searching for it—even in this form—in music; it cannot bloom there: ignorant of irony, music proceeds not from the pranks of the intellect but from the tender or vehement nuances of Naïveté, stupidity of the sublime, heedlessness of the infinite. . . . *Wit* having no equivalent in sound, we denigrate a musician by calling him *intelligent.* This attribute diminishes him and is not suitable in that languorous cosmogony where, like a blind god, he improvises one universe after another. If he were conscious of his gift, of his genius, he would succumb to pride; but he is not responsible for it; born in the oracle, he cannot understand himself. Let the sterile interpret him: he is not a critic, as God is not a theologian.

Limit-case of unreality and the absolute, infinitely real fiction, a lie more authentic than the world, music loses its prestige as soon as, dry or morose, we dissociate ourselves from the Creation, and Bach himself seems no more than insipid rumors; this is the extreme point of our non-participation in things, of our coldness and our collapse. *To jeer amid the sublime*—sardonic victory of the *subjective principle,* and one which makes us members of the Devil's brood! Lost is the man who has no more tears for music, who lives now only by the memory of those he has shed: sterile lucidity will have vanquished ecstasy—which once created worlds. . . .

The Automaton

I breathe out of prejudice. And I contemplate the spasm of ideas, while the Void smiles at itself. . . . No more *sweat* in space, no more life; the least vulgarity will make it reappear: a second's waiting will suffice.

When we perceive ourselves existing we have the sensation of a stupefied madman who surprises his own lunacy and vainly seeks to give it a name. Habituation blunts our amazement at being: we *are*—and move on, we go back to our place in the asylum of the existing.

A conformist, I live, I try to live, by imitation, by respect for the rules of the game, by horror of originality. An automaton's resignation: to affect a pretense of fervor and secretly to laugh at it; to bow to conventions only to repudiate them on the sly; to be numbered in every ledger but to have no residence in time; to save face whereas it would be only duty to lose it. . . .

The man who scorns everything must assume an air of perfect dignity, deceive the others and even himself: thereby he will the more easily accomplish his task of *counterfeit living*. What use displaying your failure when you can feign prosperity? Hell lacks *manners*: it is the exasperated image of a frank and uncouth man, it is the earth conceived without one superstition of elegance and civility.

I accept life out of politeness: perpetual rebellion is in bad taste, as is the sublimity of suicide. At twenty we rage against the heavens and the filth they hide; then we grow tired of it. The tragic attitude suits only an extended and ridiculous puberty; but it takes a thousand ordeals to achieve the histrionics of detachment.

The man who, liberated from all the principles of custom, lacks any gift as an actor is the archetype of wretchedness, the ideally unhappy being. No use constructing this model of ingenuousness: *life is tolerable only by the degree of mystification we endow it with*. Such a model would be the immediate ruin of society, the "pleasure" of communal life residing in the impossibility of giving free rein to the infinity of our ulterior motives. It is because we are all impostors that we endure each other. The man who does not consent to lie will see the earth shrink under his feet: we are *biologically* obliged to the false. No moral hero who is not childish, ineffectual, or inauthentic; for true authenticity is the flaw in fraud, in the proprieties of public flattery and secret defamation. If our fellow men could be aware of our opinions about them, love, friendship, and devotion would be forever erased from the dictionaries; and if we had the courage to confront the doubts we timidly conceive about ourselves, none of us would utter an "I" without shame. Masquerade rules all the living, from the troglodyte to the skeptic. Since only the respect for appearances separates us from carrion, it is death to consider the basis of things, of beings; let us abide by a more agreeable nothingness: our constitution tolerates only a certain dosage of truth. . . .

Let us keep deep down inside a certitude superior to all the others: life has no meaning, it *cannot* have any such thing. We should kill ourselves on the spot if an unlooked for revelation persuaded us of the contrary. The air gone, we should still breathe; but we should immediately smother if the joy of inanity were taken from us. . . .

On Melancholy

When we cannot be delivered from ourselves, we delight in devouring ourselves. In vain we call upon the Lord of Shades, the bestower of a precise curse: we are invalids without disease, and reprobates without vices. Melancholy is the *dream state of egoism*: no longer any object outside oneself, no reason for hate or love, but that same fall into a languid mud, that same circling of the damned without a hell, those same reiterations of a zeal to perish. . . . Whereas sadness is content with a circumstantial context, melancholy requires a debauch of space, an infinite landscape in order to spread out its sullen and vaporous grace, its shapeless evil, which, fearing to recover, dreads any limit to its dissolution and its undulation. It expands—strangest flower of self-love—among the poisons from which it extracts its vital juices and the vigor of all its failures. Feeding on what corrupts it, melancholy hides, under its melodious name, Self-Commiseration and the Pride of Defeat. . . .

The Thirst for Power

A Caesar is closer to a village mayor than to a mind sovereignly lucid but lacking the instinct of domination. The important fact is to command: almost all men aspire to this. Whether you have in your hands an empire, a tribe, a family, or a servant, you deploy your talent as a tyrant, glorious or absurd: a whole world or a single person obeys your orders. Thus is established the series of calamities which rise from the need, the thirst to excel. . . . We jostle none but satraps: each of us—according to his means—seeks out a host of slaves or is content with just one. No one is self-sufficient: the most modest of men will always find a friend or a companion to authenticate his dream of authority. The man who obeys will be obeyed in his turn: the victim will become the executioner; this is the supreme desire—universally. Only beggars and sages do not experience it; unless theirs is an even subtler game. . . .

The thirst for power permits History to renew itself and yet to remain basically the same; religions try to oppose this appetite, but manage only to exasperate it. Christianity would have found an issue whether the earth was a desert or a paradise. Under the variable forms man can assume is concealed one constant, an identical basis which explains why, against all the appearances of change, we move in a circle—and why, if we lost, following some supernatural intervention, our quality as monsters and clowns, history would immediately vanish.

Try to be free: you will die of hunger. Society tolerates you only if you are successively servile and despotic; it is a prison without guards—but from which you do not escape without dying. Where to go, when you can live only in the city and you lack the instincts for doing so, and when you are not enterprising enough to beg your bread, nor balanced enough to give yourself up to wisdom? In the end, you stay there like everyone else, pretending to busy yourself; you convince yourself of this extremity by the resources of artifice, since it is less absurd to simulate life than to live it.

As long as men have the passion of the city, a disguised cannibalism will rule there. The political instinct is the direct consequence of Sin, the immediate materialization of the Fall. Each man should be assigned to his solitude, but each man keeps an eye on that of everyone else. Angels and bandits have their leaders; how could the intermediary creatures—the very texture of humanity—lack theirs? Take away their desire to be slaves or tyrants and you demolish the city in the wink of an eye. The monkey-pact is sealed forever; and history follows its course, the horde gasping between crimes and dreams. Nothing can arrest it: even those who execrate it participate in its progress. . . .

Position of the Poor

Owners and beggars: two categories which oppose any change, any renewing disorder. Placed at the two extremities of the social ladder, they fear any modification in good and evil: they are equally *settled,* the former in opulence, the latter in destitution. Between them are located—anonymous sweat, the basis of society—those who strive, labor, persevere, and cultivate the absurdity of hope. The State feeds on their anemia; the notion of citizen would have neither content nor reality without them, any more than luxury and alms: the rich man and the beggar are parasites of the poor, the Pauper's dependents.

If misery has a thousand remedies, poverty has none. How succor those who persist in not dying of hunger? God himself could not correct their lot. Between fortune's darlings and the tatterdemalion circulate these honorable starvelings, exploited by splendor and by rags, pillaged by those who, loathing labor, settle, according to their luck or their vocation, in the salon or the gutter. And so humanity advances: with a few rich men, with a few beggars—and with all its poor. . . .

3

FACES OF
DECADENCE

A civilization begins to decline the moment Life becomes its sole obsession. Epochs of apogee cultivate *values* for their own sake: life is only a means of realizing them; the individual is not aware of living, he *lives*—happy slave of the forms he engenders, tends, and idolizes. Affectivity dominates and fills him. No creation without the resources of "feeling," which are limited; yet for the man who experiences only their wealth, they seem inexhaustible: this illusion *produces* history. In decadence, affective drying-up permits only two modalities of feeling and understanding: sensation and idea. Now, it is by affectivity that we participate in the world of values, that we project a vitality into categories and norms. The activity of a productive civilization consists in drawing ideas out of their abstract nothingness, in *transforming concepts into myths*. The transition from the anonymous individual to the conscious individual has not yet been made; yet it is inevitable. Measure it: in Greece, from Homer to the sophists; in Rome, from the austere old Republic to the "wisdoms" of the Empire; in the modern world, from the cathedrals to eighteenth-century lace.

A nation cannot create indefinitely. It is called upon to give expression and meaning to a sum of values which are exhausted with the soul which has begotten them. The citizen wakens from a productive hypnosis; the reign of lucidity begins; the masses wield no more than empty categories. *Myths turn back into concepts*: that is decadence. And the consequences make themselves felt: the individual *wants* to live, he converts life into finality, he elevates himself to the rank of a minor exception. The ledger of these exceptions, constituting the deficit of a civilization, prefigures its effacement. Everyone achieves delicacy—but is it not the radiant stupidity of the dolts which accomplishes the work of the great periods?

According to Montesquieu, at the end of the Empire the Roman army consisted entirely of cavalry. But he neglects to supply us with the reason for this. Imagine the legionary saturated with glory, wealth, and debauchery after having traversed countless lands and having lost his faith and his force on contact with so many temples and vices—imagine such a man *on foot*! He has conquered the world as an infantryman; he will lose it on horseback. Indolence invariably reveals a physiological incapacity to adhere any longer to the myths of the City. The emancipated soldier and the lucid citizen succumb to the barbarian. The *discovery* of Life annihilates life.

When an entire nation, at various levels, is in search of rare sensations, when, by the subtleties of taste, it complicates its reflexes, it has acceded to a fatal pitch of superiority. Decadence is merely instinct gone impure under the action of consciousness. Hence we cannot overestimate the importance of gastronomy in the existence of a collectivity. The *conscious* act of eating is an Alexandrian phenomenon; barbarism *feeds*. Intellectual and religious eclecticism, sensual ingenuity, aestheticism, and the learned obsession of good living are the various signs of one and the same form of mind. When Gabius Apicius explored the African coast for lobsters, without settling anywhere because he found none to his taste, he was a contemporary of the uneasy souls who worshipped the host of alien gods without finding satisfaction or rest among them. *Rare sensations—diverse deities*, parallel fruits of the same dryness, of the same curiosity without inner resources. Christianity appeared: a *single God*—and *fasting*. And an age of triviality and the Sublime began. . . .

A nation dies when it no longer has the strength to invent new gods, new myths, new absurdities; its idols blur and vanish; it seeks them elsewhere, and feels alone before unknown monsters. This too is decadence. But if one of these monsters prevails, another world sets itself in motion, crude, dim, intolerant, until it exhausts its god and emancipates itself from him; for man is free—and sterile—only in the interval when the gods die; slave—and creative—only in the interval when, as tyrants, they flourish.

To meditate upon one's sensations—to *know* one is eating—is an accession of consciousness by which an elementary action transcends its immediate goal. Alongside intellectual disgust develops another, deeper and more dangerous: emanating from the viscera, it ends at the severest form of nihilism, the nihilism of repletion. The bitterest considerations cannot compare, in their effects, with the vision following an opulent banquet. Every meal which exceeds, in time, a few minutes and, in dishes, the necessities disintegrates our certitudes. Culinary abuse and satiety destroyed the Empire more pitilessly than the Oriental sects and the ill-assimilated Greek doctrines. We experience an authentic shudder of skepticism only around a copious table. The Kingdom of Heaven must have represented a temptation after such excesses or a deliciously perverse surprise in the monotony of digestion. Hunger seeks a way to salvation in religion; satiety, a poison. To be "saved" by viruses, and, in the indiscrimination of prayers and vices, to flee the world and wallow in it by the same action . . . that is indeed the apex of acrimony and of Alexandrianism.

There is a *plenitude of decline* in every overripe civilization. Instincts slacken; pleasures dilate and no longer correspond to their biological function; the voluptuous becomes an end in itself, its prolongation an art, the avoidance of orgasm a technique, sexuality a science. Methods and literary inspirations to multiply the channels of desire, the imagination tormented in order to diversify the preliminaries of release, the mind itself involved in a realm alien to its nature and over which it should have no purchase—all so many symptoms of the impoverishment of the blood and the morbid intellectualization of the flesh. Love conceived as a *ritual* makes the intelligence sovereign in the empire of stupidity. Our automatisms suffer for it; shackled, they lose that impatience to let loose an inadmissible contortion; the nerves become the theater of lucid discomforts and shudders, *sensation* in short extends beyond its crude duration thanks to the skill of two torturers of studied voluptuousness. They are *the individual who deceives the species* and the blood too tepid to stun the mind, the blood chilled and thinned by ideas, *the rational blood.* . . .

*

Instincts eroded by conversation. . . .

Nothing monumental has ever emerged from dialogue, nothing explosive, nothing "great." If humanity had not indulged in *discussing* its own strength, it would never have exceeded Homer's vision, and his models. But dialectics, ravaging the spontaneity of reflexes and the spirit of myths, has reduced the hero to a tottering example. Today's Achilles has more than a heel to worry about. . . . Vulnerability, once partial and of no consequence, has become the accursed privilege, the essence of each being. Consciousness has made its way everywhere, residing in the very marrow of our bones; hence man no longer lives in existence, but in the *theory* of existence. . . .

The clear-sighted person who understands himself, explains himself, justifies himself, and dominates his actions will never make a memorable gesture. *Psychology* is the hero's grave. The millennia of religion and reasoning have weakened muscles, decisions, and the impulse of risk. How keep from scorning the enterprises of glory? Every act over which the mind's luminous malediction fails to preside represents a vestige of ancestral stupidity. Ideologies were invented only to give a luster to the leftover barbarism which has survived down through the ages, to cover up the murderous tendencies common to all men. Today we kill in the name of something; we no longer dare do so spontaneously; so that the very executioners must invoke motives, and, heroism being obsolete, the man who is tempted by it solves a problem more than he performs a sacrifice. *Abstraction* has insinuated itself into life—and into death; the "complexes" seize great and small alike. *From the* Iliad *to psychopathology*—there you have all of human history.

In civilizations on the wane, twilight is the sign of a noble punishment. What ecstasy of irony they must experience upon seeing themselves excluded from Becoming, after having established for centuries the norms of power and the criteria of taste! With each of them, a whole world goes out. Sensations of the last Greek, the last Roman! Who can keep from falling in love with the great sunsets? The charm of agony surrounding a civilization, after it has confronted every problem and marvelously warped them, offers more seductions than the inviolate ignorance by which that civilization began.

Each civilization represents an answer to the questions the universe proposes; but the mystery remains intact; new civilizations, with new curiosities, will come to try their luck, quite as vainly, each of them being merely a *system of mistakes*. . . .

At the apogee, we beget values; at twilight, worn and defeated, we abolish them. Fascination of decadence—of the ages when the truths have no further life . . . when they pile up like skeletons in the desiccated, pensive soul, in the boneyard of dreams. . . .

How dear to me that Alexandrian philosopher named Olimpius, who hearing a voice singing the Hallelujah in the Serapion, went into exile forever! This was toward the end of the fourth century; already the lugubrious stupidity of the Cross was casting its shadows across the Mind.

Around the same period, Palladas the grammarian could write: "We Greeks are no more than ashes today. Our hopes are buried like those of the dead." And this is true for all intellects of that time.

Vainly a Celsus, a Porphyry, a Julian the Apostate strives to halt the invasion of that nebulous Sublime which overflows the catacombs: the apostles have left their stigmata in men's souls and multiplied their ravages in the cities. The age of the great Ugliness begins; hysteria without quality spreads over the world. Saint Paul—the most considerable vote-canvasser of all time—has made his tours, infesting the clarity of the ancient twilight with his epistles. An epileptic triumphs over five centuries of philosophy! Reason is confiscated by the fathers of the Church!

And if I were to look for the most mortifying date for the mind's pride, if I were to scan the inventory of intolerances, I would find nothing comparable to the year 529, when, following Justinian's decree, the School of Athens was closed. The right to decadence being officially suppressed, *to believe* became an obligation. . . . This is the most painful moment in the history of Doubt.

When a nation no longer has any prejudice in its blood, its sole resource remains its will to disintegrate. Imitating music, that discipline of dissolution, it makes its farewells to the passions, to lyric waste, to sentimentality, to blindness. Henceforth it can no longer worship without irony: the *sense of distances* will be its lot forever.

Prejudice is an organic truth, false in itself but accumulated by generations and transmitted: we cannot rid ourselves of it with impunity. The nation that renounces it heedlessly will then renounce itself until it has nothing left to give up. The duration of a collectivity and its consistency coincide with the duration and consistency of its prejudices. The Oriental nations owe their everlastingness to their loyalty to themselves: having failed to "develop," they have not betrayed themselves; and they have not *lived* in the sense in which life is conceived by civilizations *on the run*, the only ones history is concerned with; for history, discipline of dawns and of gasping deathbeds—history is a novel laying claim to rigor and which draws its substance from the archives of the blood. . . .

Alexandrianism is a period of skilful negations, a style of in-utility and refusal, a display of erudition and sarcasm above the confusion of values and beliefs. Its ideal space would be at the intersection of Hellas and bygone Paris, the meeting place of the agora and the salon. A civilization evolves from agriculture to paradox. Between these two extremes unfolds the combat of barbarism and neurosis; from it results the unstable equilibrium of creative epochs. This combat is approaching its close: all horizons are opening without any being able to excite an exhausted and disabused curiosity. It is then up to the enlightened individual to flourish in the void—up to the intellectual vampire to slake his thirst on the vitiated blood of civilizations.

Must we take history seriously, or stand on the sidelines as a spectator? Are we to see it as a struggle toward a goal or the celebration of a light which intensifies and fades with neither necessity nor reason? The answer depends on our degree of illusion about man, on our curiosity to divine the way in which will be resolved that mixture of waltz and slaughterhouse which composes and stimulates his becoming.

There is a *Weltschmerz*, a *mal du siècle*, which is merely the illness of a generation; there is another which follows upon all historical experience and which becomes the unavoidable conclusion for the time to come. This is what the French call *vague à l'âme*, a melancholy yearning for the end of the world. Everything changes its aspect, even the sun; everything ages, even disaster. . . .

Incapable of rhetoric, we are romantics of lucid disappointment. Today, Werther, Manfred, René know their disease and display it without ceremony. Biology, physiology, psychology—grotesque names which, suppressing the naïveté of our despair and introducing analysis into our songs, bring us to scorn all declamation. Disciplined by the various *Treatises*, our scholarly acerbities explain our shames and classify our frenzies.

When consciousness succeeds in sounding all our secrets, when our misery has been drained of its last vestige of mystery, will we still have any fever and exaltation left to contemplate the wreck of existence and of poetry?

To bear the weight of history, the burden of becoming and that load under which consciousness sags when it considers the sum and the inanity of past or possible events. . . . In vain nostalgia invokes an impulse ignorant of the lessons taught by all that has ever been; there is a weariness for which the future itself is a cemetery, a potential cemetery as is everything which awaits being. The centuries have grown heavy and weigh upon the moment. We are more corrupt than all the ages, more decomposed than all the empires. Our exhaustion interprets history, our breathlessness makes us hear the death rattle of nations. Chlorotic comedians, we prepare ourselves for the stand-in parts in the hackneyed stories, the well-worn periods: the curtain of the universe is moth-eaten, and through its holes we see nothing, now, but masks and ghosts. . . .

The mistake of those who apprehend decadence is to try to oppose it whereas it must be encouraged: by developing it exhausts itself and permits the advent of other forms. The true harbinger is not the man who offers a system when no one wants it, but rather the man who precipitates Chaos, its agent and incense-bearer. It is vulgar to trumpet dogmas in extenuated ages when any dream of the future seems a dream or an imposture. To make for the end of time with a flower in one's buttonhole—the sole comportment worthy of us in time's passage. A pity there is no such thing as a Last Judgment, no occasion for a great defiance! Believers: hamfatters of eternity; faith: craving for a timeless *stage*. . . . But we unbelievers, we die with our decors, and too tired out to deceive ourselves with blazonry promised to our corpses. . . .

According to Meister Eckhart, *divinity* precedes God, being His essence, his unfathomable depth. What should we find at man's inmost core which defines his substance in opposition to the divine essence? *Neurasthenia*—which is to man what divinity is to God.

We live in a climate of exhaustion: the act of creation, of making and producing, is less significant in and of itself than in relation to the void, to the fall which follows. . . . For our invariably compromised efforts, the divine and inexhaustible depths are situated outside the field of our concepts and our sensations. Man was born with the vocation of fatigue: when he adopted the vertical posture and thereby diminished his possibilities of *support*, he was doomed to weaknesses unknown to the animal he was. To carry on two legs so much substance and all the disgusts related to it! The generations accumulate weariness and transmit it; our fathers bequeath to us a patrimony of anemia, reserves of discouragement, resources of decomposition, and an energy in dying which becomes more powerful than our instincts to live. And it is in this fashion that the habitude of disappearing, propped on our capital of fatigue, will permit us to realize, in the prolix flesh, neurasthenia—our essence. . . .

No need to believe in a truth to sustain it nor to love a period to justify it, every principle being demonstrable and every event legitimate. The sum of phenomena—whether fruits of the mind or of time—can be embraced or denied according to our mood of the moment: arguments, proceeding from our rigor or from our whims, are of equal weight on each point. Nothing is indefensible—from the absurdest proposition to the most monstrous crime. The history of ideas, like that of deeds, unfolds in a meaningless climate; who could in good faith find an arbiter who would settle the litigations of these anemic or bloodthirsty gorillas? This earth, a place where we can confirm anything with an equal likelihood: here axioms and frenzies are interchangeable; impulses and collapses are identified; exaltations and depravities participate in the same movement. Show me a single *case* in support of which nothing can be found. . . . The advocates of hell have no fewer claims on the truth than those of heaven—and I should plead the cause of madman and sage with the same fervor. Time deals corruption to all that manifests itself, all that acts: an idea or an event, becoming real, assumes a countenance and . . . disintegrates. Hence, when the mob of beings was stirred, History was the result, and with it the one pure desire it has inspired: that it come to an end, one way or another.

Too mature for new dawns, and having included too many centuries to crave more, all that remains for us is to wallow in the slag of civilizations. The march of time now seduces only the callow and the fanatic. . . .

We are the great invalids, overwhelmed by old dreams, forever incapable of utopia, technicians of lassitude, gravediggers of the future, horrified by the avatars of the Old Adam. The Tree of Life will no longer have spring as one of its seasons: so much dry wood; out of it will be made coffins for our bones, our dreams, and our griefs. Our flesh inherited the smell of lovely carrion scattered in the millennia. Their glory fascinated us; we exhausted it. In the Mind's graveyard lie the principles and the formulas: the Beautiful is defined, and interred there. And like it the True, the Good, Knowledge, and the Gods—they are all rotting there. (History: a context in which the capital letters decompose, and with them, the men who imagine and cherish them.)

. . . I stroll there. Under this cross Truth sleeps its last sleep; beside it, Charm; further on, Rigor; and over a host of slabs covered with deliriums and hypotheses rises the mausoleum of the Absolute; in it lie the false consolations and the deceptive zeniths of the soul. But, still higher, crowning this silence, soars Error—and halts the steps of the funereal sophist.

Since man's existence is the most considerable and the strangest venture nature has known, it is inevitable that it should also be the shortest; its end is foreseeable and desirable: to extend it indefinitely would be indecent. Having entered upon the risks of his exception, the paradoxical animal will still play, for centuries and even for millennia, his last card. Must we complain of that? No question that he will never equal his past glories, nothing suggests that his possibilities will some day provoke a rival for Bach or for Shakespeare. Decadence is first manifest in the arts; "civilization" survives their decomposition a certain time. Such will be man's case: he will continue his exploits, but his spiritual resources will have dried up, as will his freshness of inspiration. The thirst for power and domination has taken over too much of his soul: when he is master of all, he will be none the more so of his own end. Not yet being the possessor of all the means to destroy and to destroy himself, he will not perish forthwith; but it is indubitable that he will create for himself an instrument of total annihilation before discovering a panacea, which moreover does not appear to be one of nature's possibilities. He will annihilate himself as a creator—are we to conclude that all men will vanish from the earth? We must not look at the situation through rose-colored glasses. A good proportion, the survivors, will linger on, a race of subhumans, gate-crashers of the apocalypse. . . .

The imagination readily conceives a future in which men will exclaim in chorus: "We are the last: weary of the future, and even wearier of ourselves, we have squeezed out the juice from the earth and stripped bare the heavens. Neither spirit nor matter can still nourish our dreams: this universe is as desiccated as our hearts. No substance remains anywhere: our ancestors bequeathed us their tattered soul and their worm-eaten marrow. The venture is at an end; consciousness is expiring; our songs have fallen still; there gleams the sun of the dying!"

If, by accident or miracle, words were to disappear, we should be plunged into an intolerable anguish and stupor. Such sudden dumbness would expose us to the cruelest torment. It is the use of concepts which makes us masters of our fears. We say: Death—and this abstraction releases us from experiencing its infinity, its horror. By baptizing events and things, we elude the Inexplicable: the mind's activity is a salutary deception, a conjuring trick; it allows us to circulate in a tempered reality, comfortable and inexact. To learn to wield concepts—unlearn to look at things. . . . Reflection was born on a day of evasion; the consequence was verbal splendor. But when we return to ourselves and we are alone—*without the company of words*—we rediscover the unqualified universe, the pure object, the naked event; where find the boldness to face them? We no longer speculate about death, we *are* death; instead of embellishing life and assigning it goals, we strip it of its finery and reduce it to its true meaning: *a euphemism for Evil.* The grand expressions—fate, misfortune, disgrace—lose their luster; and it is then that we see the creature at grips with failing organs, vanquished under a prostrate and dumbfounded substance. Take the lie of Misery away from man, give him the power to look under this word: he cannot, for one moment, endure *his* misery. It is abstraction, sonorities without content, swollen and dilapidated, which have kept him from foundering, and not his religions and instincts.

When Adam was expelled from paradise, instead of vituperating his persecutor, he busied himself baptizing things: this was his sole way of accommodating himself to them and forgetting them; the basis of idealism was established. And what was only a gesture, a defense reaction in the first stammerer became theory in Plato, Kant, and Hegel.

In order not to be overwhelmed by our accident, we convert even our name into an entity: how can we die when we are called Peter or Paul? Each of us, more attentive to the immutable appearance of his name than to the fragility of his being, gives himself up to an illusion of immortality; once the articulation blurs, we are quite alone; the mystic who weds silence has renounced his creature condition. Imagine him, further, without faith—a nihilist mystic—and we have the disastrous consummation of the earthly venture.

. . . It is only too natural to think that man, weary of words, impatient with the iterations of time, will debaptize things and cast their names and his own into a great auto-da-fé that will engulf his hopes. We all race toward this final model, toward man mute and naked. . . .

*

I feel Life's age, its old age, its decrepitude. For incalculable epochs, Life has circled the surface of the globe by the miracle of that false immortality which is inertia; it has lingered in the rheumatisms of Time, in that time older than itself, exhausted by a senile delirium, by the endless sifting of its moments, of its doting duration.

And I feel all the weight of the race, and I have assumed all its solitude. If only it would vanish!—but its agony extends toward an eternity of corruption. I leave each moment the latitude to destroy me: not to blush at breathing is the act of a cad. No more pacts with life, no more pacts with death: having unlearned being, I consent to be effaced. Becoming—what a crime!

Having passed through so many lungs, the air no longer renews itself. Every day vomits up its tomorrow, and I vainly try to imagine the image of a single desire. Everything is an ordeal: broken down like a beast of burden harnessed to Matter, I drag the planets.

Give me another universe—or I succumb.

All I like is the explosion and the collapse of things, the fire which provokes them and the fire which devours them. The world's duration exasperates me; its birth and its disappearance delight. . . . To live under the fascination of the virginal sun and the decrepit one; to skip the pulsations of time in order to grasp the original one and the ultimate . . . to dream of the improvisation of the stars and of their extinction; to disdain the routine of being and to rush toward the two abysses which threaten it; to exhaust oneself at the beginning and at the conclusion of the moments. . . .

Thus one discovers the Savage and the Decadent in oneself, a predestined and contradictory cohabitation: two characters suffering the same attraction for *passage*, the one of nothingness toward the world, the other of the world toward nothingness: it is the need for a double convulsion, on *the metaphysical scale*. This need is expressed, on the historical scale, in the obsession of Adam whom paradise expelled and in the obsession of the man whom earth will expel: two extremities of man's *impossibility*.

By what is "profound" in us, we are victims of every evil: no salvation so long as we still conform to our being. *Something* must disappear from our composition, some deadly spring dry up; hence there is only one way out: *to abolish the soul*, its aspirations and abysses; our dreams were poisoned by it; we must extirpate it, along with its craving for "depth," its "inner" fruitfulness, and its other aberrations. The *mind* and *sensation* will suffice; their concourse will beget a *discipline of sterility* which will preserve us from enthusiasm, from anguish. Let no "feeling" disturb us ever again, and let the "soul" become the silliest of desuetudes. . . .

4

SANCTITY AND
THE GRIMACES
OF THE ABSOLUTE

Yes, truly, it seems to me that the demons are
playing ball with my soul . . .
                              —Teresa of Avila

The Refusal to Procreate

Having exhausted his appetites, the man who approaches a limit-form
of detachment no longer wants to perpetuate himself; he loathes
surviving in someone else, to whom moreover he has nothing more to
transmit; the *species* appalls him; he is a monster—and monsters do
not beget. "Love" still holds him prisoner: an aberration among his
thoughts. In love he seeks an excuse to return to the common
condition; but the *child* seems as inconceivable to him as the family,
as heredity, as the laws of nature. With neither profession nor
lineage, he achieves—final hypostasis—his own conclusion. But far as
he may be from fecundity, a more audacious monster outstrips him:
the saint, an example at once fascinating and repellent, with whom
we are always in a false position; his own is clear: no room for doubt,
no possible dilettantism. Having reached the gilded peaks of his
disgusts, at the antipodes of Creation, he has made his nothingness
into a halo. Nature has never known such a calamity: from the
viewpoint of perpetuation, the saint marks an absolute end, a radical
denouement. To regret, like Léon Bloy, that we are not all saints is
to crave humanity's disappearance . . . *in the name of faith*! How
positive, on the other hand, the devil appears, striving to seal us to our
imperfections and laboring—despite himself, betraying his essence—
to preserve us! Root out sins and life withers at once. The follies of
procreation will one day vanish—out of weariness rather than
sanctity. Man will be exhausted less for having tended to perfection
than for having squandered himself; then he will resemble a *void
saint*, and he will be just as far from nature's fruitfulness as is this
model of fulfillment and sterility.

127

Man engenders only by remaining faithful to the general fate. Once he approaches the essence of the devil or of the angel, he becomes sterile or begets abortions. For Raskolnikov, for Ivan Karamazov or Stavrogin, love is no longer anything but an excuse to accelerate their destruction; and this very excuse vanishes for Kirilov: he no longer measures himself against men but against God. As for the Idiot or Alyosha, the fact that the one apes Jesus and the other the angels places them from the start among the impotent. . . .

But to wrest ourselves from the chain of beings and to reject the notion of ancestry or posterity is nonetheless not to compete with the saint, whose pride exceeds any earthly dimension. Indeed, under the decision by which he renounces everything, under the incommensurable exploit of such humility, is concealed a demonic effervescence: the initial point, the start of sanctity, assumes the style of a challenge hurled at the human race; subsequently the saint climbs the ladder of perfection, begins talking about love, about God, turns toward the humble, intrigues the mob—and annoys us. The fact nonetheless remains that he has thrown down his gauntlet. . . .

The hatred of the "race" and of its "genius" relates you to murderers, to madmen, to divinities, and to all the great forms of the sterile. Starting from a certain degree of solitude, you must leave off loving and committing the fascinating pollution of intercourse. The man who wants to perpetuate himself at any price is scarcely to be distinguished from the dog: he is still *nature*; he will never understand that we can endure the empire of the instincts and rebel against them, enjoy the advantages of the species and scorn them: end of the line—*with appetites*. . . . That is the conflict of the man who worships and abominates woman, supremely torn between the attraction and disgust she inspires. Hence, unable to renounce the race altogether, he resolves this conflict by dreaming, on her breast, of the desert and by mingling the scent of the cloisters with the stench of over-explicit sweat. The *insincerities of the flesh* bring him closer to the saints. . . .

Solitude of hatred . . . sensation of a god turned toward destruction, treading the spheres underfoot, slobbering on the blue of

heaven and its constellations . . . of a frenzied, filthy, unhealthy god;
the demiurge ejecting, through space, paradise, and latrines; cosmogony of delirium tremens; convulsive apotheosis in which gall
consummates the elements. . . . The creatures hurl themselves
toward an archetype of ugliness and sigh for an ideal of deformity.
. . . Universe of grimaces, jubilation of the mole, the hyena, and the
louse. . . . No horizon left, except for monsters and vermin.
Everything makes for disgust and gangrene: this globe suppurating
while the living display their wounds under the beams of that
luminous chancre. . . .

The Aesthete Hagiographer

It is no sign of benediction to have been haunted by the existence of
the saints. This obsession is tainted by a thirst for diseases and a greed
for depravities. You are disturbed about sanctity only if you have
been disappointed by the earthly paradoxes; so then you search for
others, of a stranger purport, imbued with unknown perfumes and
truths; you put your hopes in follies not to be found in everyday
sensations, follies heavy with a celestial exoticism; and so you come
up against the saints, their gestures, their temerity, their universe.
Astounding spectacle! You vow to remain here all your life, to
examine it with a voluptuous devotion, to wrest yourself from other
temptations because at last you have met with the true and the
unheard of. Behold the aesthete turned hagiographer, making his
scholarly pilgrimage. . . . He makes it without suspecting that it is
no more than a promenade and that everything in this world
disappoints, even sanctity. . . .

The Disciple of Certain Saints

There was a time when to pronounce merely the *name* of a saint, a
saint who happened to be a woman, filled me with pleasure—when I
envied the chroniclers of the convents, the intimates of so many
ineffable hysterias, so many illuminations and pallors. I considered

that to be the *secretary* of such a woman, such a saint, would constitute the highest career a mortal man could enjoy. And I would covet the confessor's role among these blessed enthusiasts, and all the details, all the secrets a Peter of Alvastra kept from us about Saint Bridget of Sweden, Henry of Nordlingen about Mechthild of Magdeburg, Raymond of Capua about Catherine of Siena, Brother Arnold about Angela of Foligno, Johann of Marienwerder about Dorothea of Montau, Clemens Brentano about Catherine Emmerich. . . . It seemed to me that a Diodata degli Ademari or a Diana of Andolo rose up to heaven by the simple glamor of their names: they gave me the *sensual* taste for another world.

When I mused on the ordeals of Rose of Lima, of Lydwina of Schiedam, of Catherine dei Ricci, and of so many others, when I thought of their refinement of cruelty toward themselves, of the deliberate mortification of their charms and graces—I detested the parasite of their pangs, the unscrupulous Bridegroom, insatiable and celestial Don Juan who had the right of first tenant in their hearts. Exasperated by the sighs and sweats of earthly love, I turned to these women, if only for their pursuit of another mode of loving. "If but one drop of what I feel," said Catherine of Genoa, "were to fall into Hell, it would forthwith transform Hell into Paradise." I waited for that drop which, had it fallen, would have found me at the end of its trajectory. . . .

Murmuring over the exclamations of Teresa of Avila, I heard her crying at the age of six, "eternity, eternity," then followed the development of her deliriums, of her devotions, of her desiccations. Nothing more captivating than the *private* revelations which disconcert the dogmas and embarrass the Church. . . . I should have liked to keep a journal of those equivocal avowals, to browse on all those suspect nostalgias. . . . It is not in a bed that the peaks of voluptuous pleasure are to be scaled: how find in mere sublunary ecstasy what the saints let you suspect in their ravishment, in their transports? Bernini has shown us the quality of their secrets in his statue of the Spanish saint in Rome, where Teresa incites us to so many considerations as to the ambiguity of her swoons. . . .

When I think again about my debts for an awareness of these

extremities of passion, these darkest yet purest raptures, and that kind of absence when the nights catch fire, when the merest blade of grass, like the stars themselves, dissolves into a voice of tonic intensity—instantaneous infinity, incandescent and sonorous as a radiant and demented god might conceive it—when I think again about all this, a single name haunts me: Teresa of Avila—and the words of one of her revelations I used to repeat to myself daily: "You must no longer speak with men but with angels."

I lived for years in the shadow of these women, these saints, believing that no poet, sage, or madman would ever equal them. I expended, in my fervor for them, all my powers of worship, my vitality in desire, my ardor in dreams. And then . . . I stopped loving them.

Wisdom and Sanctity

Of all the great sufferers, the saints are best at profiting from their sickness. Willful, unbridled natures, they exploit their own disequilibrium with violence and skill. The Savior, their model, was an example of ambition and audacity, a matchless conqueror: his insinuating force, his power to identify himself with the soul's flaws and insufficiencies allowed him to establish a kingdom beyond the reach of any mere sword. Ardent with *method*: it is this ability which was imitated by those who took him for their ideal.

But the sage, scornful of drama and display, feels quite as remote from the saint as from the reveler, knows nothing of the histrionic and forges for himself an equilibrium of disillusion and unconcern. Pascal is a saint *without temperament*: sickness has made him a little more than a sage, a little less than a saint. Which accounts for his oscillations and the skeptical shadow that follows his fervors. A *bel esprit* in the Incurable. . . .

From the sage's viewpoint, there can be no one more impure than the saint; from the saint's, no one emptier than the sage. Here we have the whole difference between the man who understands and the man who aspires.

Woman and the Absolute

"While Our Lord spoke to me and I contemplated his marvelous beauty, I noticed the sweetness and at times the severity with which his lovely and divine lips uttered the words. I desired ardently to know the color of his eyes and the proportions of his stature, that I might be able to speak of them: but never have I deserved to have such knowledge. All effort to that end is of no avail."—Saint Teresa

The color of his eyes. . . . Impurities of female sanctity! To carry the indiscretion of her sex up to Heaven itself—that is of a nature to console and compensate any man—and better still, any woman—who has remained outside the divine adventure. The first man, the first woman: that is the essence of the Fall which nothing, genius nor sanctity, will ever redeem. Who has ever seen a *new* man totally superior to the one he was? For Jesus himself, the Transfiguration may have meant only a fugitive event, a development without consequences. . . .

Between Saint Teresa and other women, then, there is no more than a difference in capacity for delirium, a question of the intensity and direction of *caprice*. Love—human or divine—levels human beings: to love a girl or to love God presupposes the *same* movement: in both cases, you follow a *creaturely* impulse. Only the *object* changes; but what interest does it offer, once it is merely a pretext for the need to worship, once God is merely one outlet among so many others?

Spain

Each nation translates the divine attributes into process in its own way, yet Spain's ardor remains unique; had the rest of the world shared it, God would be exhausted, drained, and deprived of Himself. It is in order not to vanish that he makes atheism prosper in *His* countries—out of self-defense. Fearing the flames He has inspired, He reacts against His sons, against their frenzy which diminishes Him; their love undermines His power and His authority; only unbelief leaves Him intact; it is not doubts which *erode* God, but faith. For centuries the Church has trivialized His prestige, and by making Him accessible, is preparing for Him, thanks to theology, a death without enigmas, a glossed, enlightened agony: overwhelmed by the weight of prayers, how could He help being still more so by that of explanations? He dreads Spain as He dreads Russia—and multiplies atheists in both. Their attacks at least let Him retain the illusion of omnipotence: still an attribute preserved! But the believers! Dostoyevsky, El Greco: has He ever had more feverish enemies? And how could He keep from preferring Baudelaire to John of the Cross? He fears those who see Him and those through whom He sees.

All sanctity is more or less Spanish: if God were a cyclops, Spain would be His eye.

Hysteria of Eternity

I can concede a certain relish for the Cross, but to reproduce, and daily, the stale event of Calvary—that partakes of the wondrous, the inane, and the stupid. For after all the Savior, if we abuse his prestige, is as tiresome as anyone else.

The saints were great perverts, the women among them magnificent voluptuaries. All of them—frenzied by a single idea—transformed the Cross into a vice. "Depth" is the dimension of those who cannot vary their thoughts and their appetites, and who explore a single region of pleasure and of pain.

Attentive to the fluctuation of the moments, we cannot admit an absolute event: Jesus cannot cut history in two, nor the raising of the Cross break the impartial course of time. Religious thought—a form of obsessive thought—subtracts a temporal portion from the sum of events and invests it with all the attributes of the unconditioned. This is how the gods and their sons were possible. . . .

Life is the site of my infatuations: everything I wrest from indifference I give back almost at once. This is not the saints' method: they *choose* once and for all. I live in order to leave off whatever I love; they, in order to commit themselves to a single object; I savor eternity, they sink themselves into it.

The wonders of the earth—and a fortiori those of heaven—result from a durable hysteria. Sanctity: earthquake of the heart, annihilation by dint of belief, culminating expression of fanatic sensibility, transcendent deformity. . . . Between the saved and the simple-minded there is more correspondence than between the saved and the skeptic. That is the entire distance which divides faith from knowledge without hope, from existence *without results.*

Stages of Pride

Frequenting the saints' madness, you happen to forget your limits, your chains, your burdens, and you exclaim: "I am the soul of the world; I color the universe with my flames. There will be no night from now on: I have prepared the eternal banquet of the stars; the sun is superfluous: everything shines, and the stones are lighter than angels' wings."

Then, between frenzy and contemplation: "If I am not this Soul, at least I aspire to be it. Have I not given my name to all things? Every object proclaims me, from the dungheaps to the vaults of heaven: am I not the silence and the din of things?"

. . . and, at the lowest, the intoxication past: "I am the grave of sparks, the worms' mockery, a carrion importuning heaven, a carnival parody of the Beyond, a *ci-devant* Nothing without even the privilege of ever having rotted. What perfection of the abyss have I come to, that there is no space left for me to fall in?"

Heaven and Hygiene

Sanctity: supreme product of disease; when we are well, it seems monstrous, unintelligible, and morbid to the highest degree. But let that automatic Hamletism we call Neurosis claim its dues and the heavens take shape and constitute the context of anxiety. We protect ourselves against sanctity by *taking care* of ourselves: it proceeds from a special filth of the body and of the soul. If Christianity had proposed hygiene instead of the Unverifiable, we should seek in vain for a single saint in all its history; but it has championed our wounds and our squalor, an intrinsic, phosphorescent squalor. . . .

Health: decisive weapon against religion. Invent the universal elixir: the heavens will vanish and never return. No use seducing man by other ideals: they will be weaker than diseases. God is our rust, the gradual decay of our substance: when He penetrates us, we think we are elevated, but we descend lower and lower; having reached our end, He crowns our collapse, and so we are "saved" forever. Sinister superstition, haloed cancer which has eaten away the earth for ages. . . .

I hate all gods; I am not healthy enough to scorn them. That is the Indifferent Man's great humiliation.

On Certain Solitudes

There are hearts God cannot look into without losing His innocence. Sadness began after the Creation: had the Creator ventured further into the world He would have compromised His equilibrium. The man who believes he can still die has not known certain solitudes, nor the *inevitability* of immortality perceived in certain pangs. . . .

It is our modern specialty to have localized hell in ourselves: had we preserved its old countenance, fear, sustained by two thousand years of threats, would have petrified us. There are no longer any dreads which are not transposed subjectively: *psychology* is our salvation, our subterfuge. In the old days, this world was supposed to emerge from one of the devil's yawns; today it is only a mistake of the senses, a prejudice of the mind, a vice of the emotions. We know what we can do with Saint Hildegarde's vision of the Last Judgment or Saint Teresa's of Hell; the sublime—the Sublime of horror like that of holiness—is classified by any treatise on mental diseases. And if our ills are known to us, we are not thereby exempt from visions, but we no longer believe in them. Expert in the chemistry of mysteries, we *explain* everything, even our tears. This, however, remains inexplicable: if the soul is of such little account, where does the feeling of our solitude come from? what space does it occupy? And how does it suddenly replace the huge vanished reality?

Oscillation

In vain you search for your model among human beings; from those who have gone farther than you, you have borrowed only the compromising and harmful aspect: from the sage, sloth; from the saint, incoherence; from the aesthete, rancor; from the poet, profligacy—and from all, disagreement with yourself, ambiguity in everyday things and hatred for what lives simply to live. Pure, you regret filth; sordid, seemliness; vague, vigor. You will never be anything but what you are not, and the despair of being what you are. With what contrasts was your substance imbued and what mingled genius presided over your relegation in the world? Determination to diminish yourself has made you espouse in others their appetite for collapse: in this musician, this disease; in this prophet, this defect; and in women—poets, libertines, or saints—their melancholy, their vitiated spirits, their corruption of flesh and blood and dreams. Bitterness, principle of your determination, your mode of action, and understanding, is the one fixed point in your oscillation between disgust for the world and self-pity.

Threat of Sanctity

Able to live only beyond or short of life, man is a prey to two temptations: imbecility and sanctity: sub-man and superman, never *himself*. But whereas he does not suffer from the fear of being *less* than what he is, the prospect of being *more* terrifies him. Committed to pain, he dreads its conclusion: how could he consent to founder in that abyss of perfection which is sanctity, and there lose his own control? To slide toward imbecility or toward sanctity is to let yourself be lured *outside* yourself. Yet we are not alarmed by the loss of consciousness implied by the approach of idiocy, while the prospect of perfection is inseparable from vertigo. It is by imperfection that we are superior to God; and it is the fear of losing it which makes us flee sanctity! The terror of a future in which we shall no longer be in despair . . . in which, at the term of our disasters, another, unlonged for, would appear—the terror of salvation, the terror of becoming saints. . . .

The man who adores his imperfections is frightened of a transfiguration which his sufferings might prepare for him. To vanish in a transcendent light. . . . Better then to make for the absolute of darkness, toward the comforts of imbecility. . . .

The Tilting Cross

Sublime hodgepodge, Christianity is too profound—and above all, too impure—to last any longer: its centuries are numbered. Jesus fades, from day to day; his precepts, like his mildness, vex; his miracles and his divinity make us smile. The Cross tilts: the symbol is turning back into substance . . . back into the order of that decomposition in which, without exception, honorable and unworthy things die. Two thousand years of success! A fabulous resignation on the part of the most fretful animal of all . . . but our patience is exhausted. The notion that I could—like everyone else—be sincerely Christian, if only a second, casts me into perplexity. The Savior bores me. I dream of a universe exempt from celestial intoxications, of a universe with neither Cross nor faith.

Who can fail to see the moment coming when there will be no more religion, when man, lucid and empty, will have no word on hand to designate his abyss? The Unknown will be as dull as the known; everything will lack interest and flavor. On the ruins of Knowledge, a sepulchral lethargy will make us all into specters, lunar heroes of Incuriosity. . . .

Theology

I am in a good mood: God is good; I am sullen: God is wicked; I am indifferent: He is neutral. My states confer upon Him corresponding attributes: when I love knowledge, He is omniscient, and when I worship power, omnipotent. When things seem to me to exist, He

exists; when they seem illusory, He evaporates. A thousand arguments sustain Him, and a thousand destroy; if my enthusiasms
animate Him, my sulks smother Him. We cannot form a more
variable image: we fear Him as a monster and crush him like a worm;
we idolize Him: He is Being; repel Him: He is Nothingness. Were
Prayer to supplant Gravity, it would scarcely assure His universal
duration: He would still remain at the mercy of our moments. His
fate has decided that He be unchangeable only in the eyes of the
naive or the retarded. Scrutiny reveals Him: useless cause, meaningless absolute, patron of dolts, pastime of solitaries, straw or specter
according to whether he amuses our mind or haunts our fevers.

I am generous: He swells with attributes; sour: He is heavy with
absence. I have experienced Him in all His forms. He *resists* neither
curiosity nor inspection: His mystery, His infinity declines; his luster
dims; his prestige diminishes. He is a worn costume we must strip off;
how still drape ourselves in a tattered God? His degradation, His
agony drag on through the ages; but He will not outlive us, He is
aging: His last gasps will precede ours. Once His attributes are
exhausted, no one will have the energy to forge Him new ones; and
the creature having assumed, then rejected, them will go and rejoin,
in nothingness, his loftiest invention: his Creator.

The Metaphysical Animal

If we could eliminate everything Neurosis has inscribed in the mind
and the heart, all the morbid marks it has left there, all the impure
shadows accompanying it! What is not superficial is unclean. God:
fruit of the anxiety of our guts and the gurgle of our ideas. . . . Only
aspiration to the Void saves us from that exercise of corruption which
is the act of belief. What limpidity in the Art of appearance, in the
indifference to our ends and our disasters! To think of God, to seek
Him, to invoke or to endure Him—movements of a disordered body
and a defeated mind! The nobly superficial ages—the Renaissance,
the eighteenth century—scorned religion, dismissed its rudimentary
frolics. But alas! There is a plebeian melancholy in us which darkens
our fervors and our concepts. Vainly we dream of a lace universe;

God, product of our depths, our gangrene, profanes this dream of beauty.

We are metaphysical animals by the corruption we harbor in ourselves. History of thought—procession of our lapses; life of the Mind—parade of our vertigo. When our health declines, the universe suffers for it and must follow the descending curve of our vitality.

Endlessly harping on the "why" and the "how"; tracing the Cause, and all causes, on the slightest pretext—denotes a disorder of the functions and faculties which ends in a "metaphysical delirium" —senility of the abyss, downfall of anguish, ultimate ugliness of the mysteries. . . .

Genesis of Melancholy

Every profound dissatisfaction is of a religious nature: our failures derive from our incapacity to conceive of paradise and to aspire to it, as our discomforts from the fragility of our relations with the absolute. "I am an incomplete religious animal, I suffer all ills doubly"—an adage of the Fall which man keeps repeating to comfort himself. Failing to do so, he appeals to ethics, decides to follow, at the risk of ridicule, edifying advice: "*Resolve* to be melancholy no longer," ethics replies. And man strives to enter the universe of Good, of Well-Being, of Hope. . . . But his efforts are ineffectual and *against nature*: melancholy harks back to the root of our ruin . . . melancholy is the poetry of original sin. . . .

Divagations in a Monastery

For the unbeliever, infatuated with waste and dispersion, there is no spectacle more disturbing than these ruminants of the absolute. . . . Where do they find such pertinacity in the unverifiable, so much attention in the vague, and so much ardor to apprehend it as well? I share neither their certitudes nor their serenity. They are happy, and I blame them for being so. If at least they hated themselves! but they prize their "soul" more than the universe; this false evaluation is the source of sacrifices and renunciations of an imposing absurdity. Whereas our experiences have neither sequence nor system, being at the mercy of chance and our moods, they have but one experience, always the same, of a monotony and a profundity which are *profoundly* disheartening. It is true that God is its object; but what interest can they still take in Him? Always equal to Himself, infinitely of the same nature, He never *renews* Himself; I could reflect upon Him in passing, but to fill the hours with Him! . . .

It is not yet daylight. From my cell, I hear voices, and the age-old refrains, offerings to a banal Latin heaven. Earlier in the night, steps hastened toward the chapel. Matins! Even if God Himself were to attend His own celebration I would not get out of bed on a night this cold! But in any case He *has to* exist, otherwise these sacrifices of creatures of flesh, shaking off their sloth to worship Him, would be of such insanity that reason could not endure the thought. The proofs of theology are futile compared to this exertion which perplexes the unbeliever and obliges him to attribute a meaning and a use to such efforts. Unless he resigns himself to an aesthetic perspective of these deliberate insomnias, and in the vanity of these vigils sees merely the most gigantic adventure, the quest of a Beauty of non-meaning and dread. . . . The splendor of a prayer addressed to No One! But *something* has to be: when this Probable changes into certitude, felicity is no longer a mere word, so true is it that the only answer to nothingness lies in illusion. How have they acquired this illusion, labeled, on the absolute level, *grace*? By what privilege were they led to hope what no hope in this world lets us glimpse? By what right do they install themselves in an eternity which everything denies us? By what subterfuge do these possessors —the only *true* possessors I have ever encountered—arrogate the mystery to themselves in order to delight in it thereby? God belongs to them; to attempt to sneak Him away would be futile; they themselves know nothing of the *method* by which they have taken possession. *One fine day* . . . they believed. This one was converted by a simple appeal: he believed without being conscious of it; when he was, he assumed the habit. That one suffered every torment: they ceased before a sudden light. One cannot *will* faith; like a disease, it insinuates itself in you or strikes you down; no one can command it;

and it is absurd to long for it if you are not predestined to it. You are a believer or you are not, the way you are crazy or normal. I can neither believe nor want to believe—faith, a form of madness to which I am not at all subject. . . . The unbeliever's position is quite as impenetrable as the believer's. I devote myself to the *pleasure of being disappointed*: this is the very essence of the world; above Doubt, I rank only the delight which derives from it. . . .

And I answer all these pink or chlorotic monks: "You insist to no purpose. I too have gazed upon the heavens, but I have seen nothing there. Give up trying to convince me: if I have sometimes been able to find God by deduction, I have never found Him in my heart; if I found him there, I could not follow you on your path or in your grimaces, still less in those ballets which are your masses and complines. Nothing surpasses the pleasures of idleness: if the end of the world were to come, I would not leave my bed at an ungodly hour, so how would I go running in the middle of the night to immolate my sleep on the altar of the Uncertain? Even if grace beclouded me and ecstasies made me quiver unceasingly, a few sarcasms would be enough to distract me. Oh no, you see, I would be afraid to sneer in my prayers and thereby to damn myself much more by faith than by incredulity. Spare me any further effort; in any case, my shoulders are too weary to prop heaven. . . ."

Exercise of Insubmission

How I detest, Lord, the turpitude of Your works and these syrupy ghosts who burn incense to You and resemble You! Hating You, I have escaped the sugar mills of Your Kingdom, the twaddle of Your puppets. You are the damper of our flames and our rebellions, the fire hose of our fevers, the superintendent of our senilities. Even before relegating You to a formula, I trampled Your arcana, scorned Your tricks and all those artifices which produce Your toilette of the Inexplicable. You have generously endowed me with the gall Your pity spared Your slaves. Since there is no rest but in the shadow of Your nullity, the brute finds salvation by just handing himself over to You or Your counterfeits. I don't know which is more pitiable, Your acolytes or myself: we all derive straight from Your incompetence: *pitch, patch, hodgepodge*—syllables of the Creation, of Your blundering. . . .

Of all that was attempted this side of nothingness, is anything more pathetic than this world, except for the idea which conceived it? Wherever something breathes there is one more infirmity: no palpitation which fails to confirm the disadvantage of being; the flesh horrifies me: these men, these women, offal that moans by the grace of certain spasms; no more relationship with the planet: each moment is merely a vote in the urn of my despair.

What does it matter, whether Your works leave off or continue! Your subalterns cannot complete what You ventured without genius. From the blindness into which You plunged them, they will emerge nonetheless, but will they have the strength to take revenge, and will You to defend yourself? This race is rusty, and You even rustier. Turning toward Your Enemy, I await the day when he will pilfer Your sun to hang it in another universe.

5
THE DECOR
OF KNOWLEDGE

Our truths are worth no more than those of our ancestors. Having substituted concepts for their myths and symbols, we consider ourselves "advanced"; but these myths and symbols *expressed* no less than our concepts. The Tree of Life, the Serpent, Eve, and Paradise signify as much as Life, Knowledge, Temptation, Unconsciousness. The concrete figurations of good and evil in mythology go as far as the Good and Evil of ethics. Knowledge—if it is profound—never changes: only its decor varies. Love continues without Venus, war without Mars, and if the gods no longer intervene in events, those events are neither more explicable nor less disconcerting: the paraphernalia of formulas merely replaces the pomp of the old legends, without the constants of human life being thereby modified, science apprehending them no more intimately than poetic narratives.

Modern complacency is limitless: we suppose ourselves more enlightened, more profound than all the centuries behind us, forgetting that the teaching of a Buddha confronted thousands of beings with the problem of nothingness, a problem we imagine we have discovered because we have changed its terms and introduced a touch of erudition into it. But what Western thinker would survive a comparison with a Buddhist monk? We lose ourselves in texts and terminologies: *meditation* is a datum unknown to modern philosophy. If we want to keep some intellectual decency, enthusiasm for civilization must be banished from our mind, as well as the superstition of History. As for the great problems, we have no advantage over our ancestors or our more recent predecessors: men have always known *everything,* at least in what concerns the Essential; modern philosophy adds nothing to Chinese, Hindu, or Greek philosophy. Moreover, there cannot be a *new problem,* despite our naïveté or our infatuation which would like to persuade us to the contrary. In the *play of ideas,* who ever equaled a Chinese or a Greek sophist, who was ever bolder in abstraction? All the extremities of thought were reached from the first—and in all civilizations. Seduced by the demon of the Unpublished, we forget too quickly that we are the epigones of the first pithecanthropus who bothered to reflect.

Hegel is chiefly responsible for modern optimism. How could he have failed to see that consciousness changes only its forms and modalities, but never progresses? Becoming excludes an absolute fulfillment, a goal: the temporal adventure unfolds without an aim external to itself, and will end when its possibilities of movement are exhausted. The degree of consciousness varies with the ages, such consciousness not being aggrandized by their succession. We are not more conscious than the Greco-Roman world, the Renaissance, or the eighteenth century; each period is perfect in itself—and perishable. There are privileged moments when consciousness is exasperated, but there was never an eclipse of lucidity such that man was incapable of confronting the essential problems, history being no more than a perpetual crisis, even a breakdown of *naïveté*. *Negative states*—precisely those which exasperate consciousness—are variously distributed; nonetheless they are present in every historical period; balanced and "happy," they know Ennui—the natural name for happiness; unbalanced and tumultuous, they suffer Despair and the religious crises which derive from it. The idea of an Earthly Paradise was composed of all the elements incompatible with History, with the space in which the negative states flourish.

All means and methods of knowing are valid: reasoning, intuition, disgust, enthusiasm, lamentation. A vision of the world propped on concepts is no more legitimate than another which proceeds from tears, arguments, or sighs—modalities equally probing and equally vain. I construct a *form* of universe; I believe in it, and it is the universe, which collapses nonetheless under the assault of another certitude or another doubt. The merest illiterate and Aristotle are equally irrefutable—and fragile. The absolute and decrepitude characterize the work ripened for years and the poem dashed off in a moment. Is there more truth in *The Phenomenology of Mind* than in *Epipsychidion*? Lightninglike inspiration, as well as laborious investigation, offers us definitive results—and ridiculous ones. Today I prefer this writer to that one; tomorrow will come the turn of a work I detested quite recently. The creations of the mind—and the principles which preside over them—follow the fate of our moods, of our age, of our fevers, and our disappointments. We call into question everything we once loved, and are always right and always wrong; for everything is valid—and nothing has any importance. I smile: a world is born; I frown: it vanishes, and another appears. No opinion, no system, no belief fails to be correct and at the same time absurd, depending on whether we adhere to it or detach ourselves from it.

We do not find more rigor in philosophy than in poetry, nor in the mind than in the heart; rigor exists only so long as we identify ourself with the principle or thing which we confront or endure; from outside, everything is arbitrary: reasons and sentiments. What we call truth is an error insufficiently experienced, not yet drained, but which will soon age, a new error, and which waits to compromise its novelty. Knowledge blooms and withers along with our feelings. And if we are in a position to scrutinize all truths, it is because we have been exhausted together—and because there is no more sap in us than in them. History is inconceivable outside of *what disappoints*. Which accounts for the desire to submit ourselves to melancholy, and to die of it. . . .

True knowledge comes down to vigils in the darkness: the sum of our insomnias alone distinguishes us from the animals and from our kind. What rich or strange idea was ever the work of a sleeper? Is your sleep sound? Are your dreams sweet? You swell the anonymous crowd. Daylight is hostile to thoughts, the sun blocks them out; they flourish only in the middle of the night. . . . Conclusion of nocturnal knowledge: every man who arrives at a reassuring conclusion about anything at all gives evidence of imbecility or false charity. Who ever found a single joyous truth which was valid? Who saved the honor of the intellect with daylight utterances? Happy the man who can say to himself: "Knowledge turned sour on me."

History is irony *on the move*, the Mind's jeer down through men and events. Today this belief triumphs; tomorrow, vanquished, it will be dismissed and replaced: those who accepted it will follow it in its defeat. Then comes another generation: the old belief is revived; its demolished monuments are reconstructed . . . until they perish yet again. No immutable principle rules the favors and severities of fate: their succession participates in the huge farce of the Mind, which identifies, in its play, impostors and enthusiasts, ardors and devices. Consider the polemics of each age: they seem neither motivated nor necessary. Yet they were the very life of that age. Calvinism, Quietism, Port-Royal, the *Encyclopedia*, the Revolution, Positivism, etc. . . . what a series of absurdities . . . which *had* to be, what a futile and yet fatal expense! From the ecumenical councils to the controversies of contemporary politics, orthodoxies and heresies have assailed the curiosity of mankind with their irresistible non-meaning. Under various disguises there will always be *pro* and *con*, whether apropos of Heaven or the Bordello. Thousands of men will suffer for subtleties relating to the Virgin and the Son; thousands of others will torment themselves for dogmas less gratuitous but quite as improbable. All truths constitute sects which end by enduring the destiny of a Port-Royal, by being persecuted and destroyed; then, their ruins, beloved now and embellished with the halo of the iniquity inflicted upon them, will be transformed into a pilgrimage-site. . . .

It is no less unreasonable to grant more interest to the arguments around democracy and its forms than to those which took place, in the Middle Ages, around nominalism and realism: each period is intoxicated by an absolute, minor and tiresome, but in appearance unique; we cannot avoid being contemporaries of a faith, of a system, of an ideology, cannot avoid being, in short, of our time. In order to be emancipated from that, we would require the coldness of a *god of scorn*. . . .

That History has no meaning is what should delight our hearts. Should we be tormenting ourselves for a happy solution to process, for a final festival paid for by nothing but our sweat, our disasters? for future idiots exulting over our labors, frolicking on our ashes? The vision of a paradisiac conclusion transcends, in its absurdity, the worst divagations of hope. All we can offer in excuse for Time is that in it we find some moments more profitable than others, accidents without consequence in an intolerable monotony of perplexities. The universe begins and ends with each individual, whether he be Shakespeare or Hodge; for each individual experiences his merit or his nullity *in the absolute.* . . .

By what artifice did what *seems* to be escape the control of what is not? A moment of inattention, of weakness at the heart of Nothingness: the grubs took advantage of it; a gap in its vigilance: and here we are. And just as life supplanted nothingness, life in its turn was supplanted by history: existence thereby committed itself to a cycle of heresies which sapped the orthodoxy of the void.

6

ABDICATIONS

The Rope—Underside of an Obsession—Epitaph—
Secularization of Tears—Fluctuations of the Will—
Theory of Goodness—Making Allowances—Won-
ders of Vice—The Corrupter—The Architect of the
Caves—Discipline of Atony—Supreme Erosion—At
the Obsequies of Desire—Irrefutable Disappoint-
ment—In the Secret of Moralists—Monastic Fan-
tasy—In Honor of Madness—My Heroes—The
Simple-Minded—Poverty: Mental Stimulant—In-
vocation to Insomnia—Profile of the Wicked Man
—Views on Tolerance—Sartorial Philosophy—
Among the Dregs—On an Entrepreneur of Ideas—
Truths of Temperament—Flayed Alive—Incompati-
bilities—Restoration of a Cult—We Troglodytes—
Physiognomy of a Failure—Procession of
Sub-Men—*Quousque Eadem?*

The Rope

I no longer remember how I happened to become the recipient of this confidence: "Possessing not property, projects, or even memories, I have given over future and philosophy alike, owning merely a cot on which to unlearn the sun and sighs. I remain stretched out there, and spin out the hours; around me, utensils, objects which suggest suicide, every one. The nail whispers: stick me through your heart, the trickle of blood need not alarm you. The knife insinuates: my blade is infallible; one second's decision and you have triumphed over misery and shame. The window opens of its own accord, creaking in the silence: you share the city's heights with the poor; fling yourself out, my overture is a generous one; in the wink of an eye, you will land on the pavement with the meaning—or the meaninglessness—of life in your grasp. And a rope coils as though around some ideal neck, borrowing the tone of a suppliant power: I have been waiting for you forever, I have watched your terrors, your struggles, and your rages, I have seen your rumpled sheets, the pillow where your fury gnawed, as I have heard the swearwords with which you gratified the gods. Charitable, I sympathize and offer my services. For you were born to hang yourself, like all those who disdain an answer to their doubts or an escape to their despair."

Underside of an Obsession

The notion of nothingness is not characteristic of laboring humanity: those who toil have neither time nor inclination to weigh their dust; they resign themselves to the difficulties or the doltishness of fate; they hope: hope is a slave's virtue.

It is the vain, the fatuous, and the coquettish who, dreading gray hair, wrinkles and the death rattle, fill their daily vacancy with the image of their own carrion: they cherish and despair of themselves; their thoughts flutter between the mirror and the graveyard, and discover in the jeopardized features of their faces truths as serious as those of religion. Every metaphysic begins with an anguish of the body, which then becomes universal; so that those obsessed *by frivolity* prefigure authentically tormented minds. The superficial idler, haunted by the specter of age, is closer to Pascal, Bossuet, or Chateaubriand than a *savant* quite unconcerned with himself. A touch of genius in vanity: you have the great proud man who finds death hard to deal with—who takes it as a *personal offense.* Buddha himself, superior to all the sages, was merely fatuous *on a divine scale.* He discovered death, *his* death, and, wounded, renounced everything and imposed his renunciation on others. Thus the most terrible and the most futile sufferings are begotten by that crushed pride which, in order to face up to Nothingness, transforms it, out of revenge, into Law.

Epitaph

"He had the pride never to command or to prescribe anything, anyone. Without subalterns, without masters, he neither gave nor received orders. Excluded from the empire of laws and somehow anterior to good and evil, he never made a living soul suffer. The names of things faded from his memory; he looked without seeing, listened without hearing; scents and savors vanished at the approach of his nostrils, his palate. His senses and his desires were his only slaves: hence they felt, desired nothing. He forgot happiness and misery, thirst and fear; and if he happened to recall them, he scorned to name them and thereby to sink to hope or regret. The merest gesture cost him more efforts than it would cost others to establish or overthrow a kingdom. Born weary of being born, he chose to be a shade; when, then, did he live, and by the transgression of what birth? And if, living, he wore his shroud, by what miracle did he manage to die?"

Secularization of Tears

Only since Beethoven has music addressed itself to men: before him, it was concerned only with God. Bach and the great Italians knew nothing of this descent toward the human, this false titanism which has diluted, since the Deaf Man, the purest art. The torsion of the will replaced the suavities; the contradiction of the feelings, the naïve flight; frenzy, the disciplined sigh: *heaven* having vanished from music, man was installed there. Where sin had once spread in gentle tears, it now displayed itself so that declamation overtook prayer, and the romanticism of the Fall triumphed over the harmonious dream of deposition. . . .

Bach: languor of cosmogony; a scale of tears upon which our desires for God ascend; architecture of our fragilities, positive dissolution—the highest of all—of our will; celestial ruin in Hope; the one mode of destroying ourselves without disaster, and of disappearing without dying. . . .

Is it too late to relearn such dying out? Or must we go on faltering without benefit of the organ's chords?

Fluctuations of the Will

"Do you know that furnace of the will in which nothing resists your desires, where fatality and gravitation lose their empire and vanish before the magic of your power? Certain that your gaze would revive the dead, that your hand laid upon matter would bring it to life, that stones would shudder at your touch, that every graveyard would blossom in a smile of immortality—you tell yourself: 'From now on there will be nothing but an eternal spring, a dance of wonders, and the end of all sleep. I have brought another fire: the gods pale and the creatures rejoice; consternation has seized upon the vaults, and the din has descended into the very tombs.'

". . . and the amateur of paroxysms, winded, falls silent only to resume, with the accent of quietism, words of abandon:

" 'Have you ever experienced that somnolence which is transmitted to things, that slackness which weakens the sap and suggests a triumphant—and eternal—autumn? Even as I pass all hopes drowse, flowers fade, the instincts wither: everything stops willing, everything repents of having willed. And each being whispers to me: "Let someone else have lived my life, God or garter snake. I sigh for a will to inaction, an unreleased infinity, an ecstatic atony of the elements, a hibernation in broad daylight, which would benumb everything, from hog to dragonfly. . . ." ' "

Theory of Goodness

"Since for you there is no ultimate criterion nor irrevocable principle, and no god, what keeps you from committing any and every crime?

"I find in myself as much evil as in anyone, but detesting action—mother of all the vices—I am the cause of no one's suffering. Harmless, without greed, and without enough energy or indecency to affront others, I leave the world as I found it. To take revenge presupposes a constant vigilance and a systematic mind, a costly continuity, whereas the indifference of forgiveness and contempt renders the hours pleasantly empty. All ethics represent a danger for goodness; only negligence rescues it. Having chosen the phlegm of the imbecile and the apathy of the angel, I have excluded myself from actions and, since goodness is incompatible with life, I have decomposed myself in order to be good."

Making Allowances

It requires a considerable amount of unconsciousness to devote oneself unreservedly to anything. Believers, lovers, disciples perceive only one face of their deities, their idols, their masters. The worshipper remains ineluctably naïve. Is there a pure feeling which fails to betray the mixture of grace and imbecility, a blissful admiration without an eclipse of the intelligence? The man who glimpses simultaneously all the aspects of a being or a thing remains forever undecided between impulse and stupor. Dissect any belief: what pomp of the heart—and how much turpitude underneath! Infinity dreamed of in the gutter retains, ineffaceable, its imprint, its stench. There is a notary in every saint, a grocer in every hero, a concierge inside the martyr. The depth of sighs conceals a grimace; sacrifices and devotions are mingled with the vapors of the earthly bordello. Consider love: is there a nobler outpouring, a rapture less suspect? Its shudders rival music, compete with the tears of solitude and of ecstasy: sublime, but a sublimity inseparable from the urinary tract: transports bordering upon excretion, a heaven of the glands, sudden sanctity of the orifices. . . . It takes no more than a moment of *attention* for this intoxication, shaken, to cast you back into the ordures of physiology, or a moment of fatigue to recognize that so much ardor produces only a variety of mucous. The waking state in our ravishments alters their flavor and transforms their victim into a visionary trampling ineffable pretexts. We cannot love and know at the same time, without love suffering and expiring under the mind's gaze. Search your admirations, scrutinize the beneficiaries of your worship and the profiteers of your abandons: under their most disinterested thoughts you will discover self-love, the spur of fame, the thirst for domination and power. All thinkers are action's eunuchs who take revenge for their failure by the intermediary of concepts. Born *this side* of the deed, they exalt or decry it, depending on whether they aspire to humanity's gratitude or that other form of fame: its hatred; they unduly erect their own deficiencies, their own miseries to the rank of laws, their futility to the level of a principle. Thought is as much of a lie as love or faith. For the truths are frauds and the passions odors; and ultimately there is no choice except the one between what lies and what stinks.

Wonders of Vice

Whereas a thinker requires—to dissociate himself from the world— an enormous labor of interrogations, the privilege of a flaw confers from the start a singular destiny. Vice—bestower of solitude—offers the man marked out by it the excellence of a separate condition. Consider the invert: he inspires two contradictory sentiments: disgust and admiration; his "failure" makes him at once inferior and superior to the others; he does not accept himself, constantly justifies himself, invents reasons, torn between shame and pride; yet—enthusiasts of the fatuities of procreation—we go with the herd. Woe to those who have no sexual secrets! How could we divine the fetid advantages of the aberrations? Shall we remain forever the progeniture of nature, victims of her laws, nothing but human trees?

The individual's deficiencies determine a civilization's flexibility and subtlety. Rare sensations are conducive to the mind and its vitality: the distracted instinct is located at the antipodes of barbarism. Consequently an impotent man is more complex than a brute with undisturbed reflexes, and realizes better than anyone the essence of mankind, that deserter from zoology, and is enriched by all its inadequacies, all its impossibilities. Suppress vices and flaws, take away *carnal disorders,* and you will meet no more *souls*; for what we call by that name is merely a product of inner scandals, a designation of mysterious shames, an idealization of abjection. . . .

In the depths of his naïveté, the thinker envies the possibilities of knowledge open to whatever is *contra naturam*; he believes—not without repulsion—in the privileges of "monsters". . . . Vice being a suffering and the sole form of celebrity worth the trouble, the "vicious" man has to be deeper than the common run, since unspeakably separated from the rest; he begins where the others leave off. . . .

A natural pleasure, taken in what is obvious, cancels itself out, destroys itself in its own means, expires in its actuality, whereas an unwonted sensation is a *thought out* sensation, a reflection in the reflexes. Vice attains the highest degree of *consciousness*—without the intermediary of philosophy; but the thinker requires a whole lifetime to arrive at this *affective lucidity* by which the pervert begins. Yet they resemble one another in their propensity to wrest themselves from the others, though the one strives to do so by meditation while the other merely follows the wonders of his inclination.

The Corrupter

"Where have the hours gone? The memory of a gesture, the mark of a passion, the luster of a risk, a lovely, fugitive madness—nothing of all that in your past; no delirium bears your name, no vice honors you. You have slipped through without a trace; but what was your dream, then?

"I should have liked to sow Doubt into the entrails of the globe, to imbue its substance with Doubt, to enthrone Doubt where the mind never penetrated, and before reaching the marrow of mankind, to shake the calm of stones, to introduce there the insecurity and the anguish of the heart. Architect, I would have built a temple to Ruin; preacher, revealed the farce of prayer; king, hoisted the flag of rebellion. As men cherish a secret craving to repudiate themselves, I should have provoked self-betrayal everywhere, plunged innocence into stupor, multiplied disloyalties, kept the multitude from wallowing in the compost heap of certitudes."

The Architect of the Caves

Theology, ethics, history, and everyday experience teach us that to achieve equilibrium there is not an infinity of secrets; there is only one: *submit*. "Accept a yoke," these disciplines all repeat, "and you will be happy; be *something* and you shall be released from your labors." Indeed, all is *task* here on earth: professionals of time, functionaries of respiration, dignitaries of hope, a *job* is waiting for us before we are born: our careers are prepared in the wombs of our mothers. Members of an official universe, we have to occupy a place there, by the mechanism of a rigid fate, which is left vacant only in favor of the mad; they, at least, are not constrained to have a belief, to adhere to an institution, to sustain an idea, to pursue an undertaking. Since society was constituted, those who sought to withdraw from it were persecuted or mocked. You are forgiven everything, provided you have a trade, a subtitle to your name, a seal on your nothingness. No one has the audacity to exclaim: "I don't want to do anything!" —we are more indulgent with a murderer than with a mind emancipated from actions. To multiply the possibilities of submission, to abdicate his freedom, to kill the vagabond in himself—thus has man refined his slavery and enfeoffed himself to phantoms. Even his scorns and his rebellions have been cultivated only so he can be dominated by them, serf that he is of his attitudes, his gestures, and his moods. Having left the caves, he has kept their superstition; he was their prisoner, and has become their architect. He perpetuates his primal condition with more invention and more subtlety, but at bottom, dilating or diminishing his caricature, he plagiarizes himself brazenly enough. A charlatan short of tricks, his contortions, his grimaces still deceive. . . .

Discipline of Atony

Like wax in the sun, I dissolve by day and solidify at night, an alternation which decomposes me and restores me to myself, a metamorphosis in inertia and sloth. . . . Was it here that all I have read and learned was to end, was this the goal of my vigils? Idleness has blunted my enthusiasms, slackened my appetites, enervated my fury. The man who fails to let himself go seems to me a monster: I use up my strength in the apprenticeship to abandon, and train myself in leisure, confronting my whims with the paragraphs of an Art of Putrescence.

Everywhere people who *will* . . . masquerade of steps hurrying toward mean or mysterious goals; conflicting wills; everyone wills; the mob wills; thousands bent on something, anything. . . . I cannot follow, still less defy them; I stop, stupefied: what marvel inspired them with such energy? Hallucinating mobility: in so little flesh, so much vigor and hysteria! These bacteria that no scruple can calm, that no wisdom can soothe, that no gall can disconcert. . . . They brave dangers with more aplomb than any hero: unconscious apostles of the effective, these saints of the Immediate . . . gods in the carnivals of time. . . .

I turn away, and step off the sidewalks of the world. . . . Yet there was a time when I admired the conquerors and the bees, when I very nearly hoped; but now, movement maddens me, and energy merely grieves. There is more wisdom in letting yourself be carried by the waves than in struggling against them. Posthumous to myself, I remember Time as a kind of child's play or a lapse of taste. Without desires, without the hours in which to make them bloom, I have only the assurance of having always outlived myself, a fetus devoured by an omniscient idiocy even before his eyelids opened, and stillborn of lucidity. . . .

Supreme Erosion

There is something which rivals the most sordid troll, something dirty, worn, defeated, and which provokes and at the same time disconcerts fury—a peak of exasperation and an article of every moment: the *word*, any word, and more precisely the one we make use of. I say: *tree, house, me, magnificent, stupid*; I could say anything, and I dream of a murderer of all nouns and all adjectives, of all these honorable eructations. Sometimes it seems to me they are dead and no one wants to bury them. Out of cowardice, we still consider them to be alive and go on enduring their smell without holding our noses. Yet they are not, no longer express, anything. When we think of all the mouths they pass through, all the breaths they corrupt, all the occasions on which they were offered, can we still employ a single one without being polluted?

They are tossed to us pre-chewed: yet we would not dream of swallowing food already masticated by others: the material action which corresponds to the use of words turns our stomach; yet all it takes is a moment's irritation to realize, under any word, an aftertaste of someone else's saliva.

To refresh language, humanity would have to stop talking: it would resort profitably to signs, or more effectively, to silence. Prostitution of the word is the most visible symptom of its degradation; there is no utterance intact, no pure articulation, and down to the very things signified, everything is corrupted by repetitions. Why would each generation not learn a new idiom, if only to give a new vigor to objects? How love and hate, struggle and suffer with these anemic symbols? "Life," "death"—metaphysical stereotypes, exhausted enigmas. . . . Man should create another illusion of reality and invent to this end other words, since his own lack blood and, at their stage of agony, there is no transfusion possible.

At the Obsequies of Desire

A tiny cave yawns in each cell. . . . We know where diseases set in, their site, the specific weakness of the organs; but this unspecifiable ill . . . this oppression under the weight of a thousand oceans, this desire for an ideally baleful poison. . . .

The vulgarities of renewal, the provocations of the sun, of foliage, of sap. . . . My blood disintegrates when the buds open, when the bird and the beast frolic. . . . I envy the mad, the sleeping dormouse, the bear's winters, the sage's dryness; I would exchange for their torpor my agitation, the frenzy of a vague murderer who dreams of crimes this side of blood. And more than them all, how much I envy those emperors of the decadence, sullen and cruel, who were stabbed at the height of their criminal course!

I give myself up to space like a blind man's tears. Whose will am I, who *wills* in me? I wish some demon would conceive a conspiracy against man: I would join it. Tired of participating in the obsequies of my desires, I should at last have an ideal excuse, for Ennui is the martyrdom of those who live and die for no belief.

Irrefutable Disappointment

Everything confirms it, feeds it; it crowns—knowing, unimpeachable—events, feelings, thoughts; no moment which fails to consecrate it, no impulse which fails to empower it, no reflection which fails to reinforce it. Divinity, whose kingdom is limitless, more powerful than the fatality which serves and illustrates it, hyphen between life and death, it unites, identifies, and feeds on them both. Beside its arguments and verifications, the sciences themselves seem a jumble of whims. Nothing can diminish the fervor of its distastes: what truths, flourishing in a spring of axioms, could defy its visionary dogmatism, its proud insanity? No heat of youth nor even the mind's derangement resists its certitudes, and its victories are proclaimed with one and the same voice by wisdom and by madness. Before its seamless empire, before its limitless sovereignty, our knees bend: everything begins in ignorance of it, everything ends by yielding to it; no action evades it, none fails to be led back to it. The *last word* here on earth, it alone does not disappoint. . . .

In the Secret of Moralists

When we have stuffed the universe with melancholy, all we have left to light up the mind with is joy, impossible, rare, flashing joy; and it is when we no longer hope that we suffer the fascination of hope. Life—a gift given to the living by those obsessed with death. . . . Since the direction of our thoughts is not that of our hearts, we sustain a secret inclination for all that we trample down. Say a man registers the creaking of the world's machinery: it is because he has dreamed too much of the resonance of the Spheres; failing to hear them, he abases himself to hear only the din around him. Bitter words emanate from a wounded sensibility, from an offended delicacy. The venom of a La Rochefoucauld, a Chamfort, was the revenge they took on a world designed for brutes. All gall conceals a revenge and is translated into a system: pessimism—that *cruelty of the conquered* who cannot forgive life for having deceived their expectations.

The gaiety which strikes mortal blows . . . the pleasantry which conceals the dagger under a smile . . . I think of certain ironies of Voltaire, certain retorts of Rivarol, the stinging words of Mme. du Deffand, the jeers which show through so much elegance, the aggressive frivolity of the salons, the sallies which entertain and slaughter, the bitterness contained in an excess of civility. . . . And I think of an *ideal moralist*—a combination of cynicism and lyric ardor—exalted and icy, vague and incisive, as close to Rousseau's *Rêveries* as to Laclos' *Liaisons*, or uniting in himself Vauvenargues and Sade, tact and torment. . . . Observer of *mores* in *himself*, having no need to seek elsewhere, the least attention on home grounds would show him the contradictions of life, all of whose aspects he would reflect so well that, ashamed of duplication, it would disappear. . . .

No *attention* whose exercise fails to lead to an act of annihilation: this is the fatality of observation, with all the disadvantages which derive from it for the observer, from the classical moralist down to

Proust. Everything dissolves under the searching eye: passions, long attachments, ardors are the characteristic of simple minds, faithful to others and to themselves. A touch of lucidity in the "heart" makes it the seat of feigned feelings and turns the lover into Adolphe and the discontent into René. Loving, we do not examine love; acting, we do not meditate upon action; if I study my "neighbor" it is because he has ceased to be my neighbor, and I am no longer "myself" if I analyze myself: I become an *object* along with all the rest. The believer who weighs his faith ends by putting God in the scales, and safeguards his fervor only out of fear of losing it. Placed at the antipodes of naïveté, of integral and authentic existence, the moralist exhausts himself in a vis-à-vis with himself and with others: comedian, microcosm of second thoughts, he does not endure the artifice which men, in order to live, *spontaneously* accept and incorporate in their nature. Everything seems convention: he divulges the motives of feelings and actions, he unmasks the simulacra of civilization, because he suffers at having glimpsed and gone beyond them; for these simulacra give life, they *are* life, whereas his existence, in contemplating them, strays into the search for a "nature" which does not exist and which, if it did, would be as alien to him as the artifices which have been added to it. All psychological complexity reduced to its elements, explained and dissected, involves an operation much deadlier to the operator than to the victim. We liquidate our feelings by pursuing their detours, and our impulses if we ambush their trajectory; and when we detail the movements of others, it is not they who lose their way. . . . Everything we do not participate in seems unreasonable; but those who move cannot fail to advance, whereas the observer, whichever way he turns, registers their futile triumph only to excuse his own defeat. This is because there is life only in the inattention to life.

Monastic Fantasy

Those days when women took the veil to conceal from the world, and as if from themselves, the advances of age, the diminution of their beauty, the fading of their charms . . . when men, weary of fame and ceremony, left the Court to take refuge in devotion. . . . The fashion of conversion for *discretion's* sake vanished with the seventeenth century: Pascal's shadow and Jacqueline's shade fell, like invisible glamors, over the merest courtesan, over the most frivolous beauty. But Port-Royal has been destroyed forever, and with it, the places favorable to discreet and solitary agonies. No more coquetry of the convent: where now to look, in order to soften our degradations, for a context at once dim and sumptuous? An Epicurean like Saint-Evremond imagined one to his liking, and as comforting and lax as his own *savoir-vivre*. In those days, one still had to take God into account, adjust Him to disbelief, include Him in solitude. A transaction crammed with charm, irremediably vanished! We lack cloisters as dispossessed, as vacant as our souls, in order to lose ourselves there without the attendance of the heavens, and in a purity of absent ideals, cloisters befitting the disabused angels who, in their fall, by dint of vanquished illusions, would remain still immaculate. We long for a vogue of retreats in an eternity without faith, an assumption of the habit in nothingness, an Order released from mysteries, and from which no "brother" would claim anything, disdaining his salvation even as that of others, an *Order of Impossible Salvation.* . . .

In Honor of Madness

> . . . *Better I were distract:*
> *So should my thoughts be sever'd from my griefs.*
> —*King Lear*

The exclamation is wrung from Gloucester by Lear's madness. . . . In order to *separate* ourselves from our griefs, our last resort is delirium; subject to its distractions, we no longer *meet* our afflictions: parallel to our pains and adjacent to our melancholies, we divagate in a salutary darkness. When we curse that itch called life, and when we are weary of the scabs of duration, the lunatic's assurance amid his tribulations becomes a temptation and a model: let some kind fate rid us of our reason! No escape so long as the intellect remains attentive to the heart's impulses, so long as it does not break the habit! I aspire to the idiot's nights, to his mineral sufferings, to the bliss of groaning with indifference as if they were someone else's groans, to the calvary in which we are strangers to ourselves, in which our own cries come from elsewhere, to an anonymous hell where we dance and jeer as we destroy ourselves. To live and die in the third person . . . to be exiled in myself, to dissociate myself from my name, forever distracted from the man I was . . . to attain at last—since life is endurable only at this price—the wisdom of dementia. . . .

My Heroes

When we are young we look for heroes. I have had mine: Kleist, Karoline von Günderode, Nerval, Otto Weininger. . . . Intoxicated by their suicides, I was certain that they alone had gone to the end, that they drew, in death, the right conclusion from their thwarted or fulfilled loves, from their broken minds or philosophic pain. That a man should survive his passion was enough to make him contemptible or abject in my eyes: which is to say that humanity was superfluous. I discovered in it an infinitesimal number of lofty resolutions and so much compromise with life that I turned away from it, determined to put an end to it all before I was thirty. But as the years went by, I lost the pride of youth: each day, like a lesson in humility, I reminded myself that I was still alive, that I was betraying my dreams among men rotten with . . . life. Exasperated by the expectation of no longer existing, I considered it a duty to cleave my flesh when dawn broke after a night of love, and that it was a nameless degradation to sully by memory an excess of sighs. Or, at other moments, how was one to insult duration further, when one had grasped everything in a dilation which enthrones pride in the very heavens? I thought that the only action a man could perform without shame was to take his life, that he had no right to diminish himself in the succession of days and the inertia of misery. No elect, I kept telling myself, but those who committed suicide. Even now, I have more esteem for a concierge who hangs himself than for a living poet. Man is provisionally exempt from suicide: that is his one glory, his one excuse. But he is not aware of it, and calls cowardice the courage of those who dared to raise themselves by death above themselves. We are bound together by a tacit pact to go on to the last breath: this pact which cements our solidarity dooms us nonetheless—our entire race is stricken by its infamy. Without suicide, no salvation. Strange! that death, though eternal, has not become part of our "behavior": *sole* reality, it cannot become a *vogue*. Thus, as living men, we are all *retarded*. . . .

The Simple-Minded

Consider the accent with which a man utters the word "truth," the inflection of assurance or reserve he uses, the expression of believing or doubting it, and you will be edified as to the nature of his opinions and the quality of his mind. No word is emptier; yet men make an idol of it and convert its non-meaning at once into a criterion and a goal of thought. This superstition—which excuses the vulgarian and disqualifies the philosopher—results from the encroachment of hope upon logic. You are told over and over: truth is inaccessible; yet it must be searched for, aspired to, fought over. Behold a restriction which fails to separate you from those who declare they have found it: *the main thing is to believe it is possible*: to possess truth or to aspire to it are two actions which proceed from one and the same attitude. We make an exception of one word as of another: terrible usurpation of language! I call simple-minded any man who speaks of Truth with *conviction*: it is because he has capital letters in reserve and employs them naively, without deception, without disdain. As for the philosopher, his slightest indulgence in this idolatry exposes him: the citizen in him has won out over the solitary. Hope emerging from a thought—that saddens us, or makes us smile. . . . There is an indecency about putting too much soul in such words: the childishness of any enthusiasm for knowledge. . . . And it is time that philosophy, casting discredit upon Truth, freed itself from all capital letters.

Poverty: Mental Stimulant

To keep the mind vigilant, there is only coffee, disease, insomnia, or the obsession of death; poverty contributes to this condition in equal measure, if not more effectively: terror of tomorrow as much as that of eternity, money troubles as much as metaphysical fears, exclude repose and oblivion. *All our humiliations come from the fact that we cannot bring ourselves to die of hunger.* We pay dearly for this cowardice. To be dependent on men, without the vocation of beggars! To abase ourselves before these dressed-up, lucky, infatuated marmosets! To be at the mercy of these caricatures unworthy of contempt! It is the shame of seeking anything which excites the desire to annihilate this planet, with its hierarchies and the degradations they involve. Society is not a disease, it is a disaster: what a stupid miracle that one can live in it! When we contemplate it, between rage and indifference, it becomes inexplicable that no one has been able to demolish its structure, that hitherto there have not been minds desperate and decent enough to raze it to the ground without a trace.

There is more than one resemblance between begging for a coin in the city and waiting for an answer from the silence of the universe. Avarice presides over men's hearts and over matter. Away with this stingy existence! It hoards money and mysteries: purses are as inaccessible as the depths of the Unknown. But—maybe someday that Unknown will reveal itself and open its treasuries; never, so long as there is blood in his veins, will the Rich Man unearth his wealth.
. . . He will confess his shames, his vices, his crimes: he will lie about his fortune; he will make you every confidence, hand you his life: you will not share his last secret, his pecuniary secret. . . .

Poverty is not a transitory state: it coincides with the certainty that, whatever happens, you will never have anything, that you are born on the wrong side of the circuit of goods, that you must struggle for even a breath, and conquer air itself, and hope, and sleep, and that even when society disappears, nature will be no less inclement, no less perverted. No paternal principle watched over the Creation; everywhere, buried treasures; behold the Miser as demiurge, the God on high a sly skinflint. It is He who implanted in you the terror of tomorrow: it is scarcely surprising that religion itself should be a form of this terror.

For the paupers of eternity, poverty is a kind of stimulant they have taken once and for all, without the possibility of an antidote, or a kind of innate awareness which, before any knowledge of life, could describe its inferno. . . .

Invocation to Insomnia

I was seventeen, and I believed in philosophy. What did not relate to philosophy seemed to me either a sin or slops: poets? jugglers good for the amusement of trivial women; action? imbecility in delirium; love, death? low excuses rejecting the honor of concepts. Foul odors of a universe unworthy of the mind's perfume. . . . The concrete, what an abomination! Delight or suffering, what shames! Only abstraction seemed to palpitate with life: I gave myself up to ancillary exploits lest some nobler object might make me infringe my principles and submit to the degradations of the heart. I told myself over and over: only the brothel is compatible with metaphysics; and I coveted—to escape poetry—the eyes of housemaids, the sighs of whores.

. . . when you came, Insomnia, to shake my flesh and my pride, you who transform the childish brute, give nuance to the instincts, focus to dreams, you who in a single night grant more knowledge than days spent in repose, and, to reddened eyelids, reveal yourself a more important event than the nameless diseases or the disasters of time! You made me hear the snore of health, human beings plunged into sonorous oblivion, while my solitude engrossed the surrounding dark and became huger than the night. Everything slept, slept forever. There was no dawn: I shall lie awake this way until the end of time: they will wait for me then to ask me to account for the blank space of my dreams. . . . Each night was like the others, each night was eternal. And I felt one with all those who cannot sleep, with all those unknown brothers. Like the corrupt and the fanatical, I had a secret; like them I belonged to a clan to which everything could be excused, given, sacrificed: the clan of the sleepless. I granted genius to the first-comer whose eyelids were heavy with fatigue, and admired no mind that could sleep, were it the glory of the State, of Art or of Letters. I would have worshipped a tyrant who—to take revenge on his nights—would have forbidden rest, punished oblivion, prescribed disaster and fevers.

And it was then that I appealed to philosophy; but there is no idea which comforts in the dark, no system which resists those vigils. The analyses of insomnia undo all certainties. Weary of such destruction, I came to the point of telling myself: no more vacillation, sleep or die . . . reconquer sleep or disappear. . . .

But this reconquest is no easy matter: when you come close to it, you realize how deeply you have been marked by the nights. You love? . . . your impulses will be forever corrupted; you will emerge from each "ecstasy" like a scarecrow of pleasure; you will confront the glances of your too immediate companion with a criminal countenance; you will answer her sincere gestures with the irritations of an envenomed pleasure; her innocence with a guilty poetry, for everything for you will become poetry, but a poetry of transgression. . . . Crystalline ideas, happy sequence of thoughts? You will not think any more: it will be an explosion, a lava of concepts, without consequence and without order, a vomit of aggressive concepts spewed from your guts, punishments the flesh inflicts upon itself, the mind being a victim of the humors and out of the question. . . . You will suffer from everything, and to excess: the winds will seem gales; every touch a dagger; smiles, slaps; trifles, cataclysms. Waking may come to an end, but its light survives within you; one does not see in the dark with impunity, one does not gather its lessons without danger; there are eyes which can no longer learn anything from the sun, and souls afflicted by nights from which they will never recover. . . .

Profile of the Wicked Man

What is responsible for his not having done more evil than he might or must, for his not committing murder, wreaking subtler vengeances, for not having obeyed the injunctions of the blood rushing to his head? His moods, his education? Certainly not, and still less a native goodness; but merely the presence of the idea of death. Inclined to forgive no one anything, he pardons all; the slightest insult arouses his instincts; he forgets it the next moment. Enough for him to imagine his own corpse and to apply this method to others in order to be suddenly soothed; the figure of what decomposes makes him good—and cowardly: no wisdom (nor charity) without macabre obsessions. The healthy man, proud of existing, takes his revenge, listens to his blood and his nerves, heeds his prejudices, answers, blow for blow, and kills. But the mind undermined by the fear of death no longer reacts to external solicitations: it sketches out actions and leaves them unfinished; reflects upon honor, and loses it . . . tries out passions, and dissects them. . . . This dread which accompanies its gestures enervates their vigor; its desires expire before the vision of universal insignificance. Filled with hatred by necessity, unable to be so by conviction, the plots and crimes of such a man are halted in mid-course; like all men, he conceals a murderer inside himself, but a murderer imbued with resignation, and too weary to crush his enemies or to create new ones. He dreams, forehead on his dagger, and as though disappointed, before they happen, by every crime; considered a good man by everyone, he would be wicked if he did not find it futile to be so.

Views on Tolerance

Signs of life: cruelty, fanaticism, intolerance; sighs of decadence: amenity, understanding, indulgence. . . . So long as an institution is based on strong instincts, it admits neither enemies nor heretics: it massacres, burns, or imprisons them. Stakes, scaffolds, prisons! it is not wickedness which invented them, but conviction, any utter conviction. Once a belief is established the police will guarantee its "truth" sooner or later. Jesus—once he wanted to triumph among men—should have been able to foresee Torquemada, ineluctable consequence of Christianity *translated into history*. And if the Lamb failed to anticipate the torturer of the Cross, his future defender, then he deserves his nickname. By the Inquisition, the Church proved that it still possessed enormous vitality; similarly, the kings by their "royal will." All authorities have their Bastille: the more powerful an institution, the less humane. The energy of a period is measured by the beings that suffer in it, and it is by the victims it provokes that a religious or political belief is affirmed, bestiality being the primal characteristic of any success in time. Heads fall where an idea prevails; it can prevail only at the expense of other ideas and of the heads which conceived or defended them.

History confirms skepticism; yet it *is* and *lives* only by trampling over it; no event rises out of doubt, but all considerations of events lead to it and justify it. Which is to say that tolerance—supreme good on earth—is at the same time the supreme evil. To admit all points of view, the most disparate beliefs, the most contradictory opinions, presupposes a general state of lassitude and sterility. Whence we arrive at this miracle: the adversaries coexist—but precisely because they can no longer be adversaries; opposing doctrines recognize each other's merits because none has the vigor to assert itself. A religion dies when it tolerates truths which exclude it; and the god in whose name one no longer kills is dead indeed. An absolute perishes: a vague glow of earthly paradise appears, a fugitive gleam, for intolerance constitutes the law of human affairs. Collectivities are reinforced only under tyrannies, and disintegrate in a regime of clemency; then, in a burst of energy, they begin to strangle their liberties and to worship their jailers, crowned or commoners.

The periods of fear predominate over those of calm; man is much more vexed by the absence than by the profusion of events; thus History is the bloody product of his rejection of boredom.

Sartorial Philosophy

With what tenderness, and what jealousy, my thoughts turn toward the desert fathers and toward the cynics! The abjection of owning the merest object: this table, this bed, these rags. . . . Clothes get between us and nothingness. Look at your body in a mirror: you will realize that you are mortal; run your fingers over your ribs as though across a guitar, and you will see how close you are to the grave. It is because we are dressed that we entertain immortality: how can we die when we wear a necktie? The corpse that decks itself out fails to recognize itself, and imagining eternity, appropriates that illusion. Flesh covers the skeleton, clothes cover the flesh: subterfuge of nature and of man, instinctive and conventional deceptions: a *gentleman* cannot be kneaded of clay and dust. . . . Dignity, decency—so many escapes in the face of the irremediable. And when you put on a hat, who would say that you have sojourned among entrails or that the worms will gorge on your fat?

. . . This is why I shall abandon these rags and, casting away the mask of my days, flee the time when, in collusion with the others, I strive to betray myself. There was a time when solitaries stripped themselves of everything, in order to identify with themselves; in the desert or in the street, delighting in their nakedness, they attained to the supreme fortune: they were the equals of the dead. . . .

Among the Dregs

To console myself for the remorse of sloth, I take the path to the lower depths, impatient to degrade myself and identify with the gutter. I know these grandiloquent, stinking, sneering bums; engulfed in their filth, I take my pleasure in their fetid breath no less than in their verve. Pitiless for those who succeed, their genius for doing nothing compels admiration, though the spectacle they afford is the saddest in the world: poets without talent, whores without clients, businessmen without a penny, lovers without glands, inferno of women no one wants. . . . Behold then, I tell myself, man's negative fulfillment, behold, laid bare, this being who pretends to a divine lineage, pathetic counterfeiter of the absolute. . . . Here is where he was to end, in this spitting image of himself, mud God never laid a hand on, beast no angel has a part in, infinity begotten in moans, soul risen out of a spasm. . . . I contemplate that dim despair of spermatozoa that have reached their end, these funeral countenances of the race. I am reassured: I have a way to go still. . . . Then I am frightened: shall I too fall so low? And I hate that toothless crone, this rhymer without verses, these impotents of love and affairs, these models of the dishonor of the mind and the flesh. . . . The man's eyes overwhelm me; I wanted to reap, on contact with these wrecks, a harvest of pride; I take away a shudder like the one a living man would experience who, to delight in not being dead, pilfered a coffin. . . .

On an Entrepreneur of Ideas

He tries everything, and for him everything succeeds; nothing of which he is not the *contemporary*. So much vigor in the artifices of the intellect, so much readiness to confront all the realms of the mind and of fashion—from metaphysics to movies—dazzles, must dazzle. No problem resists him, no phenomenon is foreign to him, no temptation leaves him indifferent. He is a conqueror, and has but one secret: *his lack of emotion*; nothing keeps him from dealing with anything, since he does so with no accent of his own. His constructions are magnificent, but without salt: categories swell with intimate experiences, classified as in a file of disasters or a catalogue of anxieties. Here are ranged the tribulations of man, as well as the poetry of his laceration. The Irremediable has turned into a system, even a side show, displayed like an article of common commerce, a true mass product of anguish. The public delights in it; the nihilism of the boulevard and the bitterness of the café feed on it.

Thinker without fate, infinitely empty and marvelously ample, he exploits his thought, wants it to be on every mouth. No destiny pursues him: born in the age of materialism, he would have followed its facility and given it an unimaginable extension; out of romanticism he would have constituted a Summa of reveries; appearing in the world of theology, he would have wielded God like any other concept. His skill in confronting the great problems is disconcerting: everything is remarkable, except authenticity. Basically non-poet, if he speaks of nothingness, he lacks its shudder; his disgusts are pondered; his exasperations controlled and invented after the fact; but his will, supernaturally effective, is at the same time so lucid, that he could be a poet *if he wanted to,* and I should add, a saint, if he insisted. . . . Having neither preferences nor oppositions, his opinions are accidents; one regrets that he believes in them; only the movement, the method, of his thought is of interest. Were I to hear him preach from the pulpit I would not be surprised, so true is it that he locates himself beyond all truths, masters them, so that none is necessary or organic to him. . . .

Advancing like an explorer, he conquers realm after realm; his steps no less than his thoughts are enterprises; his brain is not the enemy of his instincts; he rises above the rest, having suffered neither fatigue nor that vehement mortification which paralyzes desire. Son of a period, he expresses its contradictions, its futile dilation; and when he flung himself forward in its conquest, he employed so much pertinacity and stubbornness that his success and his renown equal those of the sword and rehabilitate the mind by means which, hitherto, were hateful or unknown to it.

Truths of Temperament

Confronting thinkers without pathos, character, and intensity, who model themselves on the forms of their time, appear others of whom we *feel* that appearing whenever, they would have been the same, themselves, unconcerned by their age, drawing their thoughts from their own depths, from the specific eternity of their flaws. They take from their environment only the surface, a few peculiarities of style, a few characteristic turns of a given development. In love with their fate, they suggest explosions, tragic and solitary fulgurations, something between apocalypse and psychiatry. A Kierkegaard, a Nietzsche, had they appeared in the most anodyne age, would have had no less tremulous, no less incendiary an inspiration. They perished in their flames; a few centuries earlier, they would have perished in those of the stake: vis-à-vis general truths, they were predestined to heresy. It matters little that one be engulfed in one's own fire or in that kindled for you: the *truths of temperament* must be paid for in one way or another. The viscera, the blood, the miseries, and the vices converge to beget them. Impregnated with subjectivity, we perceive a *self* behind each of them: everything becomes confession: a shriek of the flesh is at the source of the most banal utterance; even a theory of impersonal appearance serves only to betray its author, his secrets, his sufferings: no universality which is not his mask: even logic, everything is an excuse for his autobiography; his "self" has infested ideas, his anguish has been converted into a criterion, into the sole reality.

Flayed Alive

What life is left him robs him of what reason is left him. Trifles or scourges—the passing of a fly or the cramps of the planet—horrify him equally. With his nerves on fire, he would like the earth to be made of glass, to shatter it to smithereens; and with what thirst he would fling himself toward the stars to reduce them to powder, one by one. . . . Crime glistens in his eyeballs; his hands tighten in vain to strangle. Life is transmitted like a leprosy: too many creatures for a single murderer. It is in the nature of the man who cannot kill himself to seek revenge against whatever enjoys existing. And failing, he mopes like a damned soul infuriated by impossible destructions. A discarded Satan, he weeps, pounds his breast, bows his head; the blood he wanted to shed fails to redden his own cheeks whose pallor reflects his disgust with that secretion of hopes produced by the advancing species. His great dream was to destroy the days of Creation . . . he renounces his dream, collapses into himself, and yields to the elegy of his own failure: another order of excess is the result. His skin burns: fever fills the universe; his brain is on fire: the air is inflammable. His ills fill sidereal space; his griefs make the poles tremble. And whatever is allusion to existence, the most imperceptible breath of life, wrings from him a cry which compromises the music of the spheres and the movement of the stars.

Incompatibilities

A mind compels us only by its incompatibilities, by the tension of its movements, by the divorce of its opinions from its inclinations. Marcus Aurelius, engaged on remote expeditions, tends more toward the idea of death than toward that of the Empire; Julian, made emperor, regrets his contemplative life, envies the sages, and wastes his nights polemicizing against the Christians; Luther, with a vandal's vitality, sinks and mopes in the obsession of sin, and without finding an equilibrium between his delicacies and his crudities; Rousseau, who mistakes his instincts, lives only in the idea of his sincerity; Nietzsche, whose entire *oeuvre* is nothing but a hymn to power, drags out a sickly existence of a poignant monotony. . . .

For a mind matters only to the degree that it deceives itself as to what it wants, what it loves, or what it hates; being *several,* it cannot choose *itself.* A pessimism without raptures, an agitator of hopes without bitterness, deserves only scorn. Only the man who has no regard for his past, for propriety, logic, or consideration is worthy of our attachment: how can we love a conqueror if he fails to plunge into events with a suspicion of failure, or a thinker if he has not conquered his instinct for self-preservation? Man fallen back on his futility is no longer concerned with the desire to have a life. . . . If he were to have one, or were not—would concern the others. . . . Apostle of his fluctuations, he no longer encumbers himself with an ideal identity; his temperament constitutes his sole doctrine, and the whim of the moment his sole knowledge.

Restoration of a Cult

Having *eroded* my quality as a man, nothing is any longer of any value. Everywhere all I see are animals with an ideal that herd together to bleat their hopes. . . . Even those who did not live together are constrained to do so like ghosts, or else to what end have we conceived the "communion" of saints? In pursuit of a true solitary, I scrutinize the ages, and I find there, and envy there, only the Devil. . . . Reason banishes him, the heart craves him. . . . Spirit of lies, Prince of darkness, the Evil One, the Enemy—how sweet it is to murmur the names that flayed his solitude! And how I cherish him since his daily relegation! If only I could re-establish him in his primal state! I believe in him with all my incapacity to *believe.* His company is necessary to me: a lonely being tends toward the loneliest being—toward the One. . . . I owe it to myself to tend toward him: my power to admire—fearing to remain unemployed—compels me to it. Behold me confronting my model; attaching myself to him, I punish my solitude for not being total, I forge out of it another which transcends it: it is my way of being *humble*. . . .

We replace God as best we can; for every god is good, provided he perpetuates in eternity our desire for a crucial solitude. . . .

We Troglodytes

Values do not accumulate: a generation contributes something *new* only by trampling on what was unique in the preceding generation. This is even more the case in the succession of centuries: the Renaissance could not "save" the depth, the phantoms, the genre of savagery of the Middle Ages; the Enlightenment in its turn preserved only the sense of the universal from the Renaissance, without the pathos which marked its physiognomy. The modern illusion has plunged man into the swoons of becoming: he has lost his footing in eternity, his "substance." Every conquest, spiritual or political, implies a loss; every conquest is an *affirmation* . . . but a murderous one. In the realm of art—the only one in which we can speak of the *life* of the mind—an "ideal" is established only on the ruins of its predecessor: each true artist is a traitor to his forebears. . . . There is no *superiority* in history: republic-monarchy; romanticism-classicism; liberalism-autocracy; naturalism-abstraction; irrationalism-intellectualism—institutions, like currents of thought and feeling, are of equal worth. No form of mind can assume another; we are *something* only by *exclusion*: no one can reconcile order and disorder, abstraction and immediacy, impulse and fatality. The periods of synthesis are not creative: they *summarize* the fervor of the others, a confused, chaotic résumé—every eclecticism being an indication of an ending.

Every step forward is followed by a step back: this is the unfruitful oscillation of history—a stationary . . . becoming. That man should have let himself be duped by the mirage of Progress is what renders his claims to subtlety absurd. Progress? Perhaps we can find it in hygiene. . . . But anywhere else? In scientific discoveries? After all, no more than deadly glories. . . . Who, in good faith, could *choose* between the stone age and the age of modern weapons? As close to the ape in one as in the other, we scale the clouds for the same reasons we shinnied up trees: the means of our *curiosity* pure or criminal are all that have changed, and—with disguised reflexes—we are more diversely rapacious. A mere whim to accept or reject a period: we must accept or reject history *en bloc.* The notion of progress makes us all dolts on the pinnacles of time; but these pinnacles do not exist: the troglodyte who trembled with fear in the caves still trembles in the skyscrapers. Our capital of misery remains intact down through the ages; yet we have one advantage over our ancestors: that of having *invested* our capital better, since our disaster is better organized.

Physiognomy of a Failure

Monstrous dreams inhabit groceries and churches: I have come across no one who did not live in delirium. Since the merest desire conceals a source of insanity, it is enough to conform to the instinct of self-preservation to deserve the asylum. Life—a fit of lunacy throttling matter. . . . I breathe: enough to be put away. . . . Incapable of attaining to the lucidities of death, I crawl in the shadow of the days, and I yet *am* only by the will no longer to *be.* . . .

Once I thought I could crush space with a blow of my fist, play with the stars, halt time or wield it according to my whim. The great captains seemed to me the great cowards, the poets, wretched stammerers; not knowing the resistance things, men, and words offer us, and supposing I *felt* more than the universe allowed, I gave myself up to a suspect infinity, to a cosmogony resulting from a puberty unfit to end itself. . . . How easy it is to believe yourself a god by the heart, and how hard it is to be one by the mind! And with how many illusions must I have been born in order to be able to lose one every day! Life is a miracle bitterness destroys.

The interval separating me from my corpse is a wound; yet I aspire in vain to the seductions of the grave: unable to rid myself of anything, to cease breathing either, everything in me suggests that the worms will be out of work when they get to my instincts. As incompetent in life as in death, I loathe myself and in this loathing I dream of another life, another death. And for having sought to be a sage such as never was, I am only a madman among the mad. . . .

Procession of Sub-Men

Committed beyond his means, beyond his instincts, man has ended up in an impasse. He has burned his bridges . . . to catch up with his conclusion; animal without a future, he has foundered in his ideal, he has worsted himself at his own game. Having ceaselessly sought to transcend himself, he is paralyzed; and his only remaining resource is to recapitulate his follies, to expiate them, and to commit a few more. . . .

Yet there are some to whom even this resource remains forbidden: "Unaccustomed to being men," they murmur, "do we still belong to a tribe, a race, a breed? So long as we had the prejudice of life, we espoused an error which kept us on a footing with the others. . . . But we have escaped the race. . . . Our lucidity, crumbling our skeleton, has reduced us to a limp existence—invertebrate rabble stretching out on matter to corrupt it with slobber. Behold us among the slime, behold us at that laughable end where we pay for having misused our faculties and our dreams. . . . Life was not our lot: at the very moments when we were drunk with life, all our joys came from our transports above it; taking revenge, life lugs us toward its lower depths: procession of sub-men toward a sub-life. . . ."

Quousque Eadem?

Forever be accursed the star under which I was born, may no sky protect it, let it crumble in space like a dust without honor! And let the traitorous moment that cast me among the creatures be forever erased from the lists of Time! My desires can no longer deal with this mixture of life and death in which eternity daily rots. Weary of the future, I have traversed its days, and yet I am tormented by the intemperance of unknown thirsts. Like a frenzied sage, dead to the world and frantic against it, I invalidate my illusions only to irritate them the more. This exasperation in an unforeseeable universe—where nonetheless everything repeats itself—will it never come to an end? How long must I keep telling myself: "I loathe this life I idolize?" The nullity of our deliriums makes us all so many gods subject to an insipid fatality. Why rebel any longer against the symmetry of this world when Chaos itself can only be a *system* of disorders? Our fate being to rot with the continents and the stars, we drag on, like resigned sick men, and to the end of time, the curiosity of a denouement that is foreseen, frightful, and vain.